How I Learned to Sing

New and Selected Poems

For Marag,

Best wishes

Mark
Reel

London
11/6/13.

How I Learned to Sing

New and Selected Poems
Mark Robinson

Published 2013 by
Smokestack Books
PO Box 408, Middlesbrough TS5 6WA
e-mail: info@smokestack-books.co.uk
www.smokestack-books.co.uk

How I Learned to Sing: New and Selected Poems
Mark Robinson
Copyright 2013, by Mark Robinson, all rights reserved
Cover image: Lou Robinson

Typeset by EPW Print & Design Ltd, Hartlepool.
Printed and bound in the U.K. by Biddles, part of the
MPG Books Group Ltd, Bodmin & King's Lynn.

ISBN 978-0-9571722-6-5

Middlesbrough
moving forward

Smokestack Books is
represented by Inpress Ltd
www.inpressbooks.co.uk

This book is for my ancestors,
past and present, and for my family,
with love and thanks.

'The real thing is the thing that is not there'
D.W. Winnicott

'We have come here today to be plural'
Bob Perelman

'Any resemblance between the characters in this picture
and any persons, living or dead, is a miracle.'
The Three Stooges

Contents

Esperanto Anonyme

from A Balkan Exchange (2007)

The Dunno Elegies

'We were once a great race,'
she says to him. 'The Keening people. Our ancestors
worked the mines, up there in the mountain range.
Among men, sometimes you still find polished lumps
of original grief or – erupted from an ancient volcano –
a petrified clinker of rage. Yes. That came
from up there. Once, we were rich in such things…'

from Rilke's *The 10th Duino Elegy*

translated by Martyn Crucefix

Prologue

If there's a well full of stories
where does the rain come from?
Does the springtime really need you?
Does the song comfort or fool us?
Do all angels bring terror,
navvying pickaxes down the road,
ready to rebuild anything in their way?

Does the embrace outlast the arms?
What is the guilt of the river god of the blood?
Isn't it better to be a puppet than a mask?
Should we let nothing really grow into itself?

Does telling someone a secret mean
you are forever beholden?
Do dreams reduce blood pressure?
Is fat a millennial issue? Are the blues?
How can such thick necks wrestle
the known unknowns?

The known unknowns.

Can you actually hear cracks develop
in the moistest and warmest of hearts?
How do the old men keep going?
What noise will that plate make
when it stops spinning and hits the floor?

Is that a smile on the face in the carpet?
Can you doubt the skyscraping summer stars,
the chorus rising and the breakdown rush?
Will the outstretched hand catch us?
What's so good about goodbye?

The known unknowns I know you know I don't.
The unknown knowns she knows you know.

And what to do with this rage? What to do with this loss?
The known unknowns.

And that the world goes on -
How many times can you say sorry?

Dunno.

I

Angel of the North, Gateshead

What use are angels when the wind blows back
our sighs with the sand? What use this song, nosing
through undergrowth like a dog roots out smells,
tired of its own hot-blooded clichés, bored
with knowing how lost and forgetful we are
here in this reciphered, recycled world.
If we knew how terrible it would feel
to be reminded that beauty exists
just a fleet moment from the walkers' path,
in mould on a leaf or mud in a footprint,
what would we do, would breath catch or guilt grip?

No, if I were to shout, now, on this hill
above the Team Valley Business Park,
how many angels would hear it? How many
would care that my grief had blown their cover?
The change in my pocket occupies me
for a cold minute or two. The sobbing dark
chokes on my whistling, a tune that visits
and then forgets to leave. Forgive me.
I only mean to console myself.
This is a song for my mother, the past,
an echo I hear of a better world,
a trail worn out of knotted grass, folly
that pushes you on into the woods,
a place torn down that started again,
dark native mud still on its boots,
unilluminated wings stretched out.
Magpies croon and croak and try to catch it,
trees sway bare and brown, wind-blown
hedges mime the river rushing seawards
while it takes in this hopeful new song.

The angel rusts a welcome to its brothers,
its wings embrace prayers, its sore heart escapes
the buried pithead in a gasp of song,
over the seasoned museum of the land
where the worm is king, turning like a screw
in a rawlplug, a bradawl into wet bark.
The keening rises on the valley's thermals,
rolling and tumbling into low hinterland.

But there are shadows left even by angels,
where the coal sleeps soundly, silent miles down.
The wild coast between here, there, now and then
is not so solid as it used to be.
This song was only meant to warm the air.
If it could do more it would be unbearable.
There are things only angels can forgive.

II

To walk this wilderness you must commit
to the past, to taking of evidence
from the future. You must stand prepared
to stare down demons that draw strength from dirt,
the difficult to leave behind dirt.
Head Wrightson spilt blood here, ran it off
into the river and called it rust, or money.
These call centres exist. But they are blank
as acetates laid over a map in a museum,
blank as minds of reluctant students.
Bombs could fall and no adrenalin would flow.

George Stephenson's ghost stalks the corridors,
pulled in all directions by fear of kidnap.
Stockton chains him in, Darlington too and
the wrong side of the tracks by the Tyne.
He watches over business studies degrees
and daydreams of Timothy Hackworth
bashing metal up country, near enough forgotten.

They made things here. The she-devil walked here
clutching her handbag and nearly said sorry.
Suicides the Durham bank of the river
brought more than those souls washed up in Yorkshire.
Becoming angels left their heads bloated.
The streets are dotted with students hunting a pub.
The revolution will not be televised.
There is no song to this place, no rhythm,
it is all straight lines and ambient backwash.
Every call has an answer, an even tone
blanketing all the noise that once was here.
Recycled air turns solid after twelve hours
with hardly a calorie burnt away.

The beaters and welders and handtool-burners
gather by the river to fish and to watch.
They talk of bait and boredom, of long years
watching, of the buildings and the quiet
drawn like curtains over the banging they hear.
Sparks flew but a spark now would stand out,
bright on the soft stone and white wash.
This place is all curves and circles, not sparks.
When this circle reaches back to its beginning,
you can feel the bombs drop. The weights
were heavy they used to move things here.

In the offices of Tees Valley Regeneration
a model appeals to the unseen gods.
It is an idea of heaven gone mad. It is innocent
boxes and balls that nothing can balance.
The angelic welders walk around us.
They are not concerned at our planning,
give permission for nothing, just spit
on the polished floors, breathless
from their sweated effort regardless.
They make no announcements about scale,
or what shape it should be, no prototypes
or macquettes can be put under glass
to start conversations in reception.
They do not know any of the answers.
They are not waiting to be shown through.
We are left with the questions, smooth
and unrewarding to the touch as iron.
There is no give here, nothing but
resistance to be found even now.

Everything is a trap for these angels.

III

Hadrian's Wall, Housestead's Fort

The rain is running late, eighteen words for it
loose on a hillside, different tongues
boiling down what it means to be English
by clambering over some ancient stones.
The morning has blown in through a dank blur
as if covered in moss, a hangover
worming its sorry way home to sleep.

This is bleak, a line scratched into the earth
to show the angels just who's in charge,
a long wall walked in early morning mist,
catching shadows as they take human form
and try to be like us. The fields suck light
from the sky, return it into mud.
Shoulder to shoulder the hills form circles,
block out the countries we'd otherwise see.
All the angels here have swords and curses
they taught each other in the early hours.
They left few descendants to freeze here
in the grim far North, but never went home.
They dream of desert sun and of water.
All they have is rain, the endless sound of it.

What letters do they write home in their heads?
What bitter visions do they describe
from their short foreign days in the wind?
They didn't know that they were building
a heritage for a fortress empire.
They were doing what they were told, but now
they are angelic, whatever their tribe,
and they walk amongst foolhardy tourists
in their fleece-lined jackets and woolly hats,
whisper in the ears of bright young women
those eighteen words for rain, and more for love,
love that would warm the bones, the aching bones.

Is that what survives the never-ending wind,
what divides us into those on the list
and those waiting outside for a friend with clout?
Nothing else is happening here: just sheep
counting themselves to sleep, demonstrating
the random nature of migration,
as a chain-smoking Italian teenager
brings down a bird with a flick of the wrist
and an unbecoming stone's swift flight.

IV

Blackhall Rocks

From a tangle of brambles and sea fret
you can set free an overcast afternoon,
wind cheating through your jacket
and turning the dark water to crepe.
A thick line marks the end, smudged
by an index finger, and a boat follows it.
This is the edge, the very edge, my angels,
but the dark seams run on beneath,
tunnels silent but for ghosts and gas.
Clouds and co-op bags head for sea.
They have no wishes to speak of.
They want nothing more than to rest.
Down the coast they are rebuilding Seaham,
glass-fronted buildings let in more light
than the angels saw in a month alive.
Walking sticks point, and the Timberkits
practically make themselves for you.
This is the dark coast, and do not forget it.
Every shape outlined in coaldust, blue veins
running through these red unvanquished hills.
Time and the tide pile the rocks into patterns
it must have taken pit poets to name.
Much-upon-Little watches over the beach
where angels gingerly take to the water.
If they could stand alone, this is where
they would do it, by Eye Rock,
where devoted angels can see for years.
They walk here on mornings they used to work,
they talk about the back windows that looked
out onto the sea. The wind makes them cough,
though they are long dead. They sing the old songs.
They miss the black dust, they want it back.
Dogs run down from the village, desperate
for the salt wind, the unremembering sea.

V

Dalton Park/Murton

To join the Dalton angels you must drive past
terraced rows as straight as dentures,
detached from town like a retina, head
for the purple lights of the outlets, the fun.
The backs of shops open like old tallies
used to spill their wires when broken,
lorries emptying themselves into the maws.
The streets are being unmade like sick beds,
cobbles long gone but still no tarmac.
Bassi's Golden Chippy sits the top of a line
of harsh steps and jagged cuttings to the sea.
The wind feels like history. The wind hurts.
It doesn't know, and neither do the angels,
where the backs end and scrubland starts.
Something could get undone here, on these
scrappy municipal football pitches.
Someone could get their name engraved
on the war memorial even now.
The Colliery Inn still hangs on to its paint,
but it's a backyard really, to the fresh
landscaped heart of retail you head for.

Fat where muscle reigned when this land was cleared,
the reverse somehow of a hunger strike,
this place belongs now to families, not men.
Between waddling girls and their tattooed fellas,
slow moving traffic with walking sticks shops.
Old men on the surface trying on slacks,
faces veined with years of black, delighted
now that bastard pit is gone, built over.
They dream of the roof falling above them,
wake with a cough, even the young ones.
Their grandas watch them as they pass by
and are envious, in the way angels can be,
giddily, tetchily, puzzled at themselves.

When they see a coach arrive they quicken,
run towards it, to stop it, but its only
daytrippers from Durham. They keep feeling things
that are memories of when they were young,
blush at the innocence of their mistakes.

Hopeless shop girls buy their lunchtime coffee
from hapless scrunched up time-killed waitresses.
Old women open sun-dried tomato wraps
and flash right back to that first frothy coffee.
Their friends are dying but they do not know why.
This is a bargain of a bright morning,
there is no need to spoil it for everyone.

An angel rips off his shirt, spreads his wings
and feels the watery sun on his chest.

Trees exist, but not here, not yet.

VI

Dockside Road, South Bank

Down Dockside Road things divide imperfectly,
containers block entrances to hallowed ground.
The cooling towers' pinched waists leave a smudge
of grey upon grey, cack-handed, over-looked.
Curtains cover hills that linger behind
the long back gardens of Lackenby.
In South Bank the show has not changed for years.
Parmo has left his mark in graffiti
and gravity's pull on paid-for bellies.
The betting shop is the brightest thing here.
The granddads pushing prams are whey-faced ghosts
of their granddads walking down to docks
in the bright heyday. Sculptured roundabouts,
all molten steel and welders muscles,
cast in the downtime so we remember,
could tell you a thing or two. It's not true,
that story about the sign on one of them,
'Happy 30th Birthday, Grandma.'

Behind the last hoarding plastered with posters
lies the market stall of consolation.
There the angels fight over slim pickings,
crumbs roll into balls going back to dough,
a candy-pink dolphin-edged ashtray,
a 30 miles an hour sign from the estate,
a brochure for luxury detached living
with no garden, an artwork made of string
and nails on a black-painted board,
two daffodils, an oak leaf and an umbrella,
three lengths of cornicing and a loo seat.

The angels engage with messiness,
they say, but you can take it too far.
They are not here for the good of their health:
you will find them in the karaoke.

VII

Durham Cathedral

Traffic besieges the hill, would take it
were it not for some echo of restraint.
There is too much humanity here today,
such a swarm you fear nothing would stop it
should it turn ugly and decide to riot
instead of drifting from shop to shop,
family pillage a subtle pilgrimage.

Beneath these historic cobblestones is not
the beach, but a lecture in rhetoric,
a deconstruction of the newspapers
and their black and white godlessness.

The river's swell embraces the island
and earth-bound angels throng the bridges,
miners and priests mingle, a big meeting
of those whose futures have long vanished,
but who persist, who dream on.

The cathedral knocker will give refuge
but only for forty short days and nights.
It cannot keep the voices of angels out
of your head, choirs rustling down corridors,
harmonies rising like clouds that will flood
the pits in the dark so far underground.
Sediment of slack, the run-off of ages,
wrinkled faces and washhouse hands
behind the scenes still, waiting for learning.
These are lucky angels in such grand halls.
Banners and tapestries clash, purple
and crimson sit awkward together.
Songs drown each other out. Tills are loudest.

Listen to the bells. Listen to the bells
and look down onto the green, a car park
or a postage stamp on a letter to God.
Every carving, every stone laid upon stone,
sings of faith, whilst the shoppers stretch their backs
and complain they must trek down the mountain.
This is success in this world. Silence
a gargoyle's glare from the High Street.
Angels escort them back to the river.
The water is a charm full of lead and coal.
As darkness falls erudite drunks fill the streets.

VIII

Hartington Road, Stockton-on-Tees

'Just being here is glorious' (Rilke)

If terror is the first thing to marrow our bones
when we see these green hills filter the sky
what next? What comes after fear's surf breaks
on the tiny pebbles of the everyday?
One foot in front of the other until
you have forgotten that you are not normal.
A letter on a doormat. A dishcloth in the sink.
Cleaning windows on the seventh floor.
Hassan from Iraq, Apollo from the Congo,
Farooq from Sri Lanka, Betty the Afghani,
Asel who would not speak or smile,
place their feet where the Roman empire trod,
the land of Hadrian and the land of angels,
to sing of our heartening normality,
our placidness and hospitality.

Buttoning up a child's coat in a wet playground,
toggles the shape of ducks bright against the quilt,
they sing. Listening in their yards to playtime
they sing of home and home and the spaces between.
They chat over coffee to the spirits of family
who do not understand where they have arrived,
who walk through markets confused and adrift
wondering how this light makes familiar shapes
look and feel so different, so distant.
The rain goes through them like a melody
fills the house when they sing in the evenings,
folksongs from their other home, lifting them
like high winds lift tiles to put them down
gently, in the same spot, the same pattern.

All that was solid has melted into haircuts
strange and terrible, misshapen boots,
questions to be answered. But survival
means this becomes home, a place where angels
don't care if you are coming or going.
You walk through the same rain as angels,
perform your own ceremonies of thanks.

IX

Teesport, Redcar

Rolling picture of the utterly here,
land still in turmoil as markets crash,
morphing and merging in hostile arrangements
when old certainties just evaporate
like red steam leaking from pressured globes
the heart of networks of private roads.
All the power that once was here changed.
Iron made a place appear overnight,
now it is rusting the water ochre.
Ore in these dark hills, a dance in the pipe-work.
An endless mess of goods trains shuffles
through imitations of illuminations,
past stone-tongued fire-eaters and fireworks
burning messages into the heavens.
Our children wheeze, and tiny angels
keep them company in their fragile games.
This is a blank land of grey-faced fences,
barbed wire barriers and strengthened steel.
It scrubs its face raw because it is proud,
and it wants the world to be orderly.
Though the angels on the backs of trains
think it looks so shiningly chaotic
something good must come from its blissful rush,
the wind tastes bitter, chemical, beaten.
You can see its shape from Redcar beach,
nourish a warm dream of Holy Island,
so far to the North the light is different.
There is quiet there, and cleaner daylight,
permanent beside the gulls' plainsong.

But here, gates are locked, one by one
companies become simply history.
Too many to list, those that are gone.
Molten, the angels that record their names.

X

Fitness First, Eaglescliffe

I am no good at thinking. I am only good
at noting things down and putting one foot
in front of another for a long time.
That's what this gym is for, energy
passing from my legs into the treadmill
into the cold earth, the brownfield site
that lies beneath the car park and our feet.
Staring down the mirrored middle-distance
pains put to one side, and death just a myth,
this joyous suffering seeks a resting place.
I put grief aside, can think of the lost
without tears so long as I keep moving.
I think I am somehow making the earth turn.
If I do it quickly enough better words will come,
these sudden gusts of grief and remembrance
will be as welcome as wind on a beach.

Except our feet do not touch the ground,
our feet float somewhere just above the dirt.
I can hear voices, I can hear voices
in my head as I count the steps I make,
as I check off left then right then left again
then again then again then again until,
I look up at the wall of mirrors ahead
and see the angels walking the aisles
between the machines, shaking their heads.

These factory boys cannot believe us.
A room full of heat, lines of effort and hope,
calm self-deception, wild reassessment –
panting none can hear through our headphones,
or over machines' arrhythmic heartbeat
filling the eaves like a kind of song.
Glances cross in the mirror, sizing up
an undertow of exposure, openness
to anything but a conversation.
Brows dip under the weight of sweat,
heads nod, shoulders rock, into a body
of lone people not communicating.
The crescendo we do not hear gets worse.

The women angels me-mo across the rows,
lips and eyes exaggerate the clarity
of their conclusions, their bemused anger,
no more than a whisper in the room
but a metallic scream in the glass.
Endurance wasn't built in a day, it says
on the wall. They are killing themselves laughing.
They run their hands over the rails and the seats
looking for the joins, for how things are made.

My legs are moving only out of habit,
my brain frozen. A voice in my headphones speaks.

It's not the absence of the things we've lost
that redefines us, but their echo,
not a betrayal, but a warm embrace,
wings and chest calming the song to silence.
What is here suffices. So stop running.

How I Learned to Sing

As luck would have it

'I was born in a wheatfield snapping my fingers'
Tomaz Salamun

I was born in the back bedroom of a council house,
breech and purple from bruising, not picked up
for three days except when absolutely necessary.
I was born in a room that looked out over
the playing fields of my primary school.
I imagine my mum and dad, and my nan,
gripping the window ledge as eager boys below
played football while I cried and cried and cried.

I was born weeping and bursting my lungs,
as unanswered calls swept through rooms
and through houses, until the whole terrace
was holding its breath, until the Beatle-cut fathers
had to walk down the gardens in the rain
to smoke fag after slow musty fag in the dusk.

Dream/Home

From the salted mines of memory
I emerge with whole years blank,
blue with bruises to secretly press,
confuse with desire or excitement.
I palm off sweat, wipe the sky clean,
the air just moments from dirt
bouncing around my lungs
while an accident waits to happen
in the gap between brain and tongue.

Awake to drunkenness, heavy breath
swamping crows' apologies for rain.
I am orderly and neat but desperate.
The houses in the background
mutate under pressure to form
a grammatically correct sentence.
The past a suburb the greenbelt can't touch.
I am orderly and neat and the next
is a subject we really ought to drop.

Domestic comedy

The real thing is the thing that is not there.
As I walk in the room, my mother walks out.
The real thing is the thing that is not there.
As I start to speak, someone else coughs.
The real thing is the thing that is not there.
As I crack my knuckles, no one worries.
The real thing is the thing that is not there.
As I pick at woodchip, my mother hoovers.
The real thing is the thing that is not there.
As I turn each page, the telly is turned up.
The real thing is the thing that is not there.
As I flick channels, my sister pummels the sofa.
The real thing is the thing that is not there.
As I chew my lips, I make the clock tick louder.
The real thing is the thing that is not there.
As I cut a hole in his paper, my father laughs.
The real thing is the thing that is not there.
As I carry on smiling, we all carry on smiling.

Photograph now containing a line translated from Neruda

The small fire of a new planet
hidden in my parents' eyes
in a snapshot taken on a beach
the summer after I was born.
Insatiable hunger for light caught
just as it turned to something they could touch,
warm stones of the spur into the sea,
the buttons of the cardigans against sunburn,
my dad's army tattoos still blue as the sky,
mum's hips tilted like an invitation,
me squirming to get away before the photo is taken.

Mum, sometime early 70's, judging by the puff sleeves and collar

She holds the four cornets like flowers,
as if pausing on the steps of the church
for one last snapshot before marriage.

The trees are wiry and the sky cold,
the hedge still taking shape around us.
If you can be graceful and still at once,
she is, reducing everything else to a blur.

She holds herself as if
she never wanted to move again,
as if the years to come
were pounding on the back gate,
demanding a lick of our ice creams.

Diptych

The boy kicking the ball against his garden fence
is begging to be asked to play. He stares at his neighbours
doing laps of the block on their new bikes, adds
in his imagination to their whoops and yells, and sighs.
Homework sits undone on the dining table. He's not bright.
When he leaves school he stacks shelves and loves it,
chats to old women about their sons and shopping.
When he's 38 he retrains as a bus driver.

I'm counting cars to see if the rain has stopped.
If the next four cars that come over the bridge
have their wipers on then it must really be raining.
I'm not lonely enough to talk to anyone yet. I'm lost
in a game of Subbuteo cricket. Peter Lever is bowling
as fast as he possibly can. The ball keeps vanishing
under my sister's bed. I'm as happy as I will be for years.
I carefully adjust the scoreboard to read 96 for 7.

Primary

The trees at school talked to themselves
while I held firm and fierce at right back.
The dinner hall looked just like it smelt –
off white, peeling, corrugated like
the cardboard lining my grow-into shoes.
A queue of children holding chairs
two feet off the ground snaked past.
Then a sudden burning dragged me towards
a chant with two girls pulling hair at its centre.

When I got home, I stormed my sister's room,
overturned chairs, tilted pictures, stamped on dolls
crowded on her quilt, to get even, get done.
The lawn beneath her window bit its tongue.
My mum said nothing. I still have the urge
to turn over a few tidy things and see who cares.

How I learned to sing

The day spins like a plate on a pole,
sunlight streaming down and around us,
carving shadows out of the beach.
A snag of mishaps has shaped mum's face
into a taut parody of itself.
We are sent to find crabs, in pools
where we have not seen a crab for years.
The sea is a vein in the estuary,
the tide coming in a race memory,
and stranded pools dot the sand
with water still so cold it cramps
our calves before we can fight.
Then my sister is suddenly dancing,
splashing towards me with her discovery,
a small pink starfish she waves
in my dumbstruck face.
Though she is smaller, I can't reach it,
she ducks and swerves away
like the memory of it now.
I can't reach her, mum and dad
are too far back to help, but
I want that starfish, want to run
my fingers over its serrations,
pop it in my pocket to frighten
my mum with as we wipe sand
from between our toes later.
I start to scream at my sister,
first words and then just noises,
and the gulls turn from pencil flicks
to real birds with real blood
rushing beneath sharp feathers,
claws asking my shirt whether
it will rip or be carried off,
and now my voice has gone soft
and crying for what I can't get
I feel my wings rise and set,

the gulls craws and my own throat
harmonise as I pale and float
up and over the docile waves,
not worrying, or wanting to be saved,
looking down on the strip of beach
at the family I could not reach,
and singing *back back back.*

Photographer unknown

Mainland Studios,
174 Nathan Road, Kowloon,
Tel. 63959

Eighteen months of National Service have puffed out their chests.
They are all in dark suits except my Dad,
who's wearing a beautiful fawn three button job.
They are all half way down thick-ridged pints
except my dad who clutches a bottle of the local ale
that has put a blank glaze on his smooth face.

The Hong Kong sun has polished all their faces,
given them memories to take home in their chests,
but not from tonight, not after so much ale
their eyes cannot quite find the camera, Dad
staring off into the distant years, the pints
of sweat spilt back in his civvy job.

The night is yet young and it's a good job
according to the look on his mate's face,
swarthy and sleek as his finger points
aggressively or jokingly or both at the photographer's chest,
his finger echoing Kitchener or Uncle Sam on my Dad's
shoulder, his tanned face making my dad's yet more pale.

There is plenty of time to finish that ale,
every hair on their heads is slick, just the job.
They had no choice in how they got here, Dad
eighteen and bored when called up to face
whatever came along (no battles but a dead-man's chest
spilt once from a crash in the hills) so if nine pints

is what it takes, then they will take ten pints
and go off looking for the squaddie's holy grail.
But for now they're five young men with chests
strong enough for war who can forget about the job
they'll have tomorrow, scraping a hungover face
free from the sheen this photo shows it had.

I can imagine the one on the right punching my Dad
later in the night, after one too many pints
have blurred the gang the photographer faced
for his pittance, dredging up some forgotten betrayal
or some joke that should or shouldn't have come out of his gob.
But the photo and my Dad keep that tight to their chests.

Dad – I can't tell if it's damage or delight, or just ale,
that make you look alone among the pints. I'd have a job
to ask you to your face, to explain the tightness in my chest.

The toilet being downstairs, the lounge became his sick room

Damp sits on his chest and blossoms
like coral in tobacco-cured lungs
that struggle to start on cold mornings,
wan and shrinking, tight as sleep.

I nestle beneath the dining table
and close my eyes to see what he sees,
hear what he hears, drugged,
us breathing through pillowed air.

Quiet. Not absolute silence but
lights and shapes blurred like a hint
at some new kind of cinema,
atmospheres decaying to fuzz.

In the hush I trace the flowers
that push through the anaglypta,
through the rasping from the settee
from which there is no relief.

Soon my fingertips are tingling.
The tick of the clock gets louder.
The kettle starts to whistle.
He props himself up and dredges a joke:

Right then, who wants belting?
he says, just as he'd demand of us
when he burst in from steaming up
to Carlisle or down to Crewe.

We used to laugh, and hide behind the settee,
like you were supposed to
when Daleks snuck up on the Doctor,
though we never saw what was scary about that,

all he had to do was run upstairs.

The Nelson Bible

The illuminated lineage and age-greased leather
of that hand-deep Bible didn't reach our house.

Nan Nelson never forgave my Nan's remarriage.
Auntie Margaret become paraphrase, pained

by arthritis and Chinese Whispers.
We made do with a Gideon, pocket sized, in 8pt type

on paper Izal shiny, thin as my watery faith.
When sent to be confirmed it came in very handy.

My parents' empty-nesting moves lost it.
In its unremembered place I keep just

my Grandad's ASLEF badge, his silver-railed driver's cap,
a textbook, something technical to do with trains.

Laying a carpet with my Dad

We squeezed the settee out to the dining room
then rolled up the old carpet and flopped it on the stairs
to lie there till bin day like a subject we'd had to drop.

Feeding the shiny white bannister through my hands
I ran up to my room or to the loo along its back.
The foam cracked and fell off, like scabs I picked at.

The Stanley knife was so sharp I was forbidden to touch.
Along the spikes of the Betagrip I ran my fingers
till I had scratched new patterns on the tips, the prints.

We rolled out the fragrant new carpet in strict rhythm,
counting, as if learning to dance, so that it didn't slant,
revealing more of its pattern with each movement.

Dad whipped round the edges trimming the excess and then
we set to pulling and pushing it to that taut perfection
my Mum expected. Nothing of a job, but satisfying.

The knee-kicker was an instrument of torture
you could fall in love with, for the give of the cushion
as you punched it forward, the grip of the pins, silver, not
        letting go.

Dad and I would sit in the middle of the empty room
and try to ignore the corner where the carpet did not quite
        reach.
That was where we would put the settee.

Crossing the road, Mum would say,

is not like in your silly cartoons.
Once flattened, real children don't get up.
When she let go of my hand opposite
the bus stop I was Speedy Gonzalez,
small, excitable, Mexican, free.
To the newsagents for a Marathon.

At playtime I shared it with Nick Day
as we got excited over *My Dingaling*,
deaf to the bells, or the alarm
the very idea set off in our parents.
Nick sang *Long Haired Lover from Liverpool*
as if he was from Salt Lake City, not
the wrong side of the playing fields,
and a family who swore in front of him.

Standing now at that bus stop starting block
I'm married, visiting home but driven
to escape from endless photos of myself
and the lover I brought home from Liverpool,
and our children – whose hands my mother
will not drop this long Bank Holiday Weekend –
I see that highly-strung mouse re-run, sprint
the marathon over The Bridges to school,
away from his mother – *Andelez, andelez*–
all the way to his eleven-plus.

(And then, that first Grammar School morning,
newly uniformed and cardboard-briefcased,
with a tie the neighbours had never seen before,
my mother waved me off at the bus stop
to the jeers of the sixth-formers at the back.
I saw her cross the road and start to wait
for her bus to work. May she slap my backside
if I'm cutting or changing things for effect –
for I am not too big.)

Fine

There is nowhere to hide in this silence.
Dusty corners exposed, the carpet's
telltale craters smoothed down
by the settee casters or the table legs
silent as the sunlight via the nets
silent as the flames of the gas fire
patterned lino leaching into silence
the skin of the morning cracked
and crusted as cold rice pudding
which gulped down proves love
certain edges not coloured over
silence of the right sides of lines
silence of the unneeded pint
silence of overflowing magazine racks
and supplements beneath cushions
bursting with cardboard and silence
silence of the bitten tongue
silence of the frozen cheek
a moment hanging on the landing
looking down over the stairs
into silence of the tv
a badge on a lapel that says
silence is the mother of invention
silence of the advert brew
silence that mixes coffee and sugar
and melts them down to nothing
silence of the stars above the garden
overseeing pointless anger
silence of the belly and belt
silence of the nodding head
silence of my father's wrinkles
silence of my mother's tongue
the grief inside anger
inside silence inside me

Happily

I've a fraudulent centre to me,
he says, I only want a sweaty hug.
I don't care about bad breath.
His tongue is a simple one,
has only a few verbs now,
mysterious in inflexion.
One means to *arrive just in time.*
One means *go as in die.*
His hands make a cup to catch the wind in.
He throws the remnants back over his shoulder.
He listens to the buffeting rocks
in the tumbler of the wind.
Noise is a kind of desire.
He plays folk songs on his guitar,
wrinkled, sky-blue songs that brood
their way into kitchen corners
hunting that burnt-toast smell.
There are new words to them:
horribly present, happily there.

Horribly present, happily there,
listening and watching
as the sounds shrink to nothing.
He wants a word that means
disappearance of the breath
whilst dreaming of a baby
in a pram in a back-yard
but it evades him like a bus
sailing through on amber.
After the gym his muscles
are taut to the point of ping.
But that is what he wanted.
He has a small statue of himself
in the pit of his stomach,
all smooth lines and curves
but it is crying, it is melting,
softening with each day.

He says he is afraid of gravity now.
He says he is afraid of curtains,
the flesh between the shoulder
and the bicep, and lines left
around the waist by trousers.
The wrongs of it in the mirror.
He has inherited her mouth
and can see his face slowing
to a soft, shudderless halt.
She is happily there, in mirror,
children, memory, hope.

Summer job

The carpet warehouse my father walked
smelt of foam backing and sweat.
Not the fresh tang of muscled effort,
for the work was a dull queue of a day,
but the dead sheen of a thorough grounding
in the core skills of back and forth.

At dinnertime some played rummy for pennies,
thick lads honed their sequencing and always lost.
I forced gerunds into unsuitable corners
of the Tough Crossword in Dad's Mirror,
watched the congregation of porn pull staples
from a blank-faced stunner's belly button.

As dead afternoons shuffled to a close,
I'd be moved from stacking to the action end
of the cutting machine, wrapped lengths
of domestic satisfaction in brown paper,
learnt to fold over neatly, flip and tape,
then heave over and down into the van

where some poor soul had to hump
the different lengths into as solid a mass
as he could, fill up from the back.
That was one step up from the brush,
but time passed quickly. You could guess
the weight of the next one to fly towards you.

Driving home pain crackled down my fingers,
real and pleasing. 'That'll go,' my Dad said.
'Or it would if you were here long enough.'
I tried to persuade him his bosses were bastards
but he just would not, would not have it.
He kept saying I would learn.

Cultural revolution

for Howard Slater & Jim Burns

From Manchester Howard brought
Ann Charters' Kerouac biography,
a Crispy Ambulance single
and the first seeds of dissatisfaction
with major chords. He lent me
Fred Engels in Woolworths
which made even Stockport
sound like a newly fashionable
arrondissement on the left bank.
The warehouses by the canal
had only just been gutted
by unseen hands of capital.
Huge metal chains hung down
from rusting beams in monochrome.
The doors were cracked wide
and railway tracks led calmly to echoing spaces.
We wrote poems about the tenderloin
and lobsters in parks for six months,
gave up Deepdale for the cafes,
tilted our heads to parallel
the fifties sugar pourers in Brucci's.
From there, it was only a matter of time
before we were playing the bass
with the side of our thumbs, dubbing
flat vowels onto The Parallax View,
making strange connections
where there was only hope.
The deterritorialization
of the Flag Market and Europe's
biggest bus station is yet to occur.

Where thinking got me

It was ideas cut my chest tight.
The dusk sang me ragged,
wrang me dry as salt.

Hollow backed with hunger
I held the face in the mirror
steady, simple as a toy box,

while I sweat myself some air.
Three deep sweet breaths
made my young neck flush

when some sudden consolation
wrapped me in papier-mâché,
delivered me into stereo,

then made me run everything
I'd ever done again, backwards,
all the way home.

First day in the kitchen

Through the rough suede of the penultimate kiwi
the wrong knife with a too thin blade
pushed through the clatter of plates and bowls
and the rush of the clock towards lunch
and bit to the bone in a bloodless moment.

A wink of skin on my finger held
its bloody breath in the stainless glow
of steel and tile scrubbed free of grease
in the tired afternoons that followed.
So many times, with bleach and wire brush,

but I never managed the whiteness
I saw that first morning, five minutes
on a chair in the corner blushing blood red,
wondering exactly what I could rescue
from the almost perfect fruit salad.

On realising I am English

'The important thing is to adapt your dish of spaghetti
to circumstances and your state of mind.'
Guiseppe Marotta

In the parallel universe where wizened Corsicans
rave over suet dumplings and rapturously murmur
improvised sonnets in praise of stotty,
barm cake, bloomer, cob, scone (to rhyme with gone),

no one would criticise me for never mentioning
the real grievance at the heart of this poem.
I'd be lauded for the tightness of my lip,
for the way you feel my teeth grit and grind,

for how I shrug off questions with a joke
about the endless spouting of emotion
I waded through to get here.

I think this as the glaze of a first pressing
spreads its lucent green over the frying pan,
ready to spit at the very suggestion of an onion.

To prove something urgent

after a night of talk and confusion
we are running so fast for the lamppost
feet slip on the gravel longing to break skin
and suddenly I am skidding on my chin
like a lemming relishing
one last slow contact with the earth
since it is beautiful to be alive, amazing
to be lost in the dark between streetlights
wondering how the woods tripped us and why.

But the trees in the darkness wink at each other
as the theoreticians in the branches stare
and try to recall the breakthrough they made
not more than five seconds ago, not more
than five seconds ago, when they were dead
and we were not sober, not bleeding.

Loose connections beneath the dashboard

From Yarm to Netherthong on an empty tank
without adding a mile to our history,
we have guessed our speed in the suburbs,
crossed our fingers in sweaty gridlock
and cruising on the M1 listened to rattles
accumulate like guilty verdicts,
first one sorry hand, then another,
then more until it's unanimous: off with his head.
According to the car we have not moved.
The landscape was having us on,
tugging hedgerows into the distant behind-us,
the wheels were turning in air, or mud,
and this holiday cannot yet have started -
the children are still screaming to leave.
But the momentum that carried us here
must register somewhere. The wheels
could draw a map or a house or a face
without turning the clock or taking a pound,
without scratching our part-exchange,
but something has shifted, has pushed us
99 miles towards older and wiser.
Repeating this trick is a difficult knack,
one that can get you from yesterday
to now to tomorrow and back.

Return

'It is better to be in love with your wife
than to be in love with your poetry'
Toma Markov

1.
air like a lump in the throat
in this dark haired city
if a horse could lay pumpkins
they'd be like those piled high
on market stalls at Sitnyakovo
and I'd be full of ginger carrying
my swollen heart home to bake

2.
This is a long fever, secret like a wish,
pale as you and flowers in its miracle heat.
It is close to mute, and lies snug in our palms in the
            dark.

So quietly new is it even now a breath might break
to talk of heart, hope, and then hold still
while our blood runs hot again,

guessing how every dry afternoon would feel
if this flush didn't warm the air,
didn't catch us falling into balance.

3.
Of many parallel worlds
I choose this one.

Second-hand

After Exec Board I take the tube back with Michael and Laura,
talking about how colleagues can mean one thing when we mean
three others. We laugh, but in that way that suggests resignation.
They stay on to Euston but I have time to kill and no desire
for drink. Houseman's is still there, despite fresh frontages
and development, so I walk along Pentonville Road,
remembering Scala all nighters and dark 80s afternoons.
There are still dozens of black, white and red all over newspapers
at the back of the shop, but the basement's a mess,
a damp-smelling likeness of the revolution. I spot a Canongate
reissue though, of *Jack's Book*, and am innocent again,
taking that box of voices out of the village library every 6 months,
the small room to the side, for biographies and non-fiction.
(I picture Donald Wood's *Biko* in the same breath.)
That was the start of something, could have turned
a world upside down. In fiction they had *The Trial*,
Amerika, The Town and the City and *Vanity of Dulouz*
and that was just the Ks. There were only two poetry books I liked:
Selected Poems by Dylan Thomas and Leonard Cohen.
Later they got Adrian Mitchell's *For Beauty Douglas*.
I remember reading a book about Hegel, but sweet nothing
about Hegel himself, though I could sketch you the cover.
Today I am wearing a suit, but so are Jack and Neal
in some of the photos. I pay three pounds for my young self's sake,
wondering whether my thirst for ideas is slaked or not.
The bloke behind the counter upstairs is the wrong man
but takes the money anyway. He asks me where I'm from,
and then congratulates me on not living in London. He is Scottish,
he says, but doesn't sound it. I imagine he lives in London because
it is the epicenter of the turmoil to come. He ought to move
to Newton Aycliffe, I think. I feel dirty-nostalgic
leafing through as I wait for the platform to come up for the 16.00
to Aberdeen. There are lots of men in kilts and Scotland shirts,
frayed hung-over looks to them, returning from a miracle in Paris.
I spend most of the journey home working on the laptop,
looking just like someone who knows about spreadsheets,
then finish all the sudoku I can find in the *Independent*.

Untitled

Madness could sky me restless,
Come to an end in a pebble-dashed house
And the drone of autumn leaves.

This kitchen table is not made of wax.
Hear the sound my knuckles make on it
as I hunt words that could apologise enough.

Writing paper is too white, too shiny, so
I use the space around the Guardian crossword,
knowing you'll see it, will work it out.

To be alive as this and still hoping!
I don't want to lose all the good things.
But I've gone through the day

with a fine-toothed comb and eyes closed,
like a schoolboy in humid double History.
I've the time and inclination to forgive myself

but I can't. The washing up says I'm nothing.
That's not peace through the open window,
just sarcastic pity from the sunlight.

Flesh wants to break, to relax and sag.
But this kitchen table is not made of wax
and the door behind me has shut with a click.

These legs do not move up and down

of their own accord, but following
the pattern of the plosives in an altercation
I once had with a shopkeeper in Redcar
about the slack nature of his avocados.
This causes me to skip slightly in damp weather,
but has otherwise added a pleasingly
assertive edge to my bandy gait.

For years I had based my jerky progress
on some vowel sounds on precious black vinyl,
but this I see now had held me up no end.
If I could I would start again from the beginning,
but be calmer, take up yoga and breathing.

I shall now translate this poem
into small circular movements
which will gradually edge me out of here.

Work/life balance

Breathing in and breathing out feels like a game –
my eyes just pits of 6am,
my tongue furred with precision-
tooled caveats that fold into an equation
the mirror flings back
in my face – I'm knackered.

Four vodkas slapped me to sleep before
the news raised its fists and I woke
to the world going mad, quite
mad, and felt as if I had been caught.
If being human was so bloody easy
everyone would be doing it.

Tomorrow I will shout myself hoarse
watching North End kick Sunderland's arse.

2nd sestina for Alan Robinson,
a Deepdale Finnale

I march as if catching up, feet off the ground
across every gutter from the bus station, my Dad
swerving me through ginnels he used to walk
with his gang from Lady Street, demolished now, toward a win,
but only for the police horses on the terraces as we lose,
then make our way back through fight-littered streets

that now glow in the dark, suddenly glamorous streets -
one set of expectations drowning another, grounds
for a Saturday night on the tiles as I lose
him in the crowd, squeeze back to the barrier and there's Dad
leant where he can hardly see, dreaming of pools wins
and telling his friend the boss exactly where to walk,

how one day we'd drive there, stop short to walk
from Nan's penultimate nursing home through streets
a shimmer of redbrick fresco into sunlit wind,
make our way across Moor Park's muddy ground
hopeful and joking, sometimes with my Mum, Dad's
being dragged there something we did together, lost

when her legs would not support her, when to simply lose
was harder than it had ever been to make that slow walk
through optimism and renewal, to find in my Dad
imagined grit of those proud sheepish workers' streets
turned into short lets, passing through drugged ground
where the roar for late equalisers sounds like a win

to wretched early leavers too eagerly taking wing,
his shot knees cracking shut to slow him, mine loose
as ever, dragging *my* son now, hopeful that the ground
floodlit ahead might hold a game that would let us walk
away brightly, with only praise, only laughter, through streets
rivering with victors around us as we wait for Granddad,

eddies of history, generations of anticipation, all that Dad
disdained to climb so high to see, an echo of a Finney win
blowing these foggy memory-streaked streets,
full of everything all of us will one day lose,
someone who remembers the ancient trail we walk
towards who knows what, away from the very ground

that taught Dad how to teach me to lose
the desire to always win, to find a line to walk
through tight-woven streets, mapping hearts' home ground.

*Finnale: ancient Lancastrian verse form, a sestina mentioning
Sir Tom Finney*

Not quite good enough

to eat, there's a thread in this morning
that I will hold onto
while my descant ploughs it to mud.
Nowhere is as nowhere does,
its shape at the back of my throat
a cry, grain, a frayed response soon
wordless,

all texture and no text,
in the sunlight or the rain,
the gap between truth and harmony,
now and here two halves of nowhere.

For my love

I will bring vodka, ice and lime and pray for rain,
kumquats and ask for forgiveness.

There is a light falling suggestively on the street,
a cold, blond light from years ago in another country.

There were statues in the park with warmer hands than mine
when I plucked yours from your pockets and squeezed.

Such a long time ago now, and nothing to be done,
which is why I bring you fruit and drink and hope.

Yin/Yang Bounce – 12 line blues

A watershed in its blitheness
your face this winter's morning
stirs me still, reverses discord,
a moment's shapely turn as
one thing runs into another
and we barely pause.

                    Later
we won't mention it, we'll blush
and know why the other is blushing,
will push on through, a horn section
waiting for the simple teamwork
of a rousing head arrangement,
then out.

Cooking

I heard a trumpet honour
the smoking wok of our love.
My hands were full but patient,
my heart gone contrapuntal,
and blood did what it had to
to keep alive and moving,
and even with domestic flames
the pan was red and smoking
and garlic, chilli, ginger couldn't
make this moment hotter,
garlic, chilli, ginger would just
sizzle, spit and burn.

Billie dancing, 11

You step from the wings
            a memory caught in light
leap sure as a heartbeat
away and back and hold my breath

Ribbon curl of quick arms
            twists around the music
a balance of heel then off
away and back and hold my breath

Invincible upon the line
            your dash across our lives
a swift kind of poise
away and back and hold my breath

Your body's fresh world
            dreams in circles then jumps
and rolls off into dark
away and back and hold my breath

Yet more mine you hop away
            leave my breath trapped tight
your eyes stare down the dark
away and back and hold my breath

'My son, already disappearing into a man'

(Caroline Forché)

– forgive me. Let the basketball hoop
slip this caught breath through. Let
Granddad's painted model Jag chip
back to green in the Airfix drawer.
Let car boot aliens wait away 15p lives
in a broken tangle of headphones.
Let skate posters fade to black and red.
Let books tessellate, heroes rewind like tapes,
Disney on flu-ridden Wednesdays.
Let the Playstation beat us. Let Scalextric
click together and form a virtuous circle
to hum us into conversation.
Let broccoli yellow in the fridge.
Let your paintings grow away from you,
embarrassing in the bathroom.
Let the day get longer. Yes, let the days get longer.
Let small boys gaze at you in wonder as your bike
goes higher than their heads in The Dippers.
Let me and Mum walk past you in the street
and let you and your friends not see us.
Let dusk go unremarked for the first time,
the tree house fall in unnailled chunks
under leaves till Spring, your name sprayed
in primary school red, like a plaque on the lawn.
Let the homework rows be forgotten.
Let the twisted guitar strings rust. Let
the broken guitar in the attic stay there,
superglued neck and impossible fingerings
silent but for the breeze-hum only the varnish
and dust can hear. Let how it got that way
go the way of all cries. Let this moment be our secret.
Let me teach you D and A and G.
Let them be enough for now. Let
this basic language have its uses. Let me be foreign
in this strange land. Let me just about get by.

10.15am in a garden in Preston-on-Tees

a small winter poem for Billie

Tired of tidiness, my OCD a running joke,
I let the washing up dry itself.

Winter holds back the weeds
through the plastic beneath the decking.
Clematis underlines your window,
reaches for the house's edge.

The goldfish in the pond is greedy.
Over the fence and the backs it is break-time.
The playground is no quieter now you are grown.
I remember you small and fierce
and wish you were home.

Instead of apologising again

You shouldn't expect me to be clearer
in my feelings than I am in my dreams.
I curl my pink baby's tongue and my tiny fists.
I've a horse in my chest called I Wonder.

If we felt the earth pulse back through our hips,
we'd forget about the handprint on the mirror,
and the holes in the cardboard bathroom wall.
The field my horse keeps down is a big one.

One curt glance home and you're still waving.
The far edge of the world remains to be seen.
Keep steady, for my horse can grow wilder
than the fresh air cut to ribbons by the wind.

Any time we've wasted we won't get back.
It's a kind of sleep my horse will not tolerate.

Going

I recall it now as it will be then:
stillness suddenly present overhead
and the earth twitching madly beneath my feet,
a Thursday beaten with sticks and sickly sweet.

I will leave behind a half hummable tune,
and messages etched in the soles of my shoes.
Brickwork kicked into chunks by the gate
suggest what happened happened too late.

A Thursday when dark fades in before three,
still years from a breath of the weekend,
I will go, eyes open, not awash with pain,
but wanting them to wish I crop up again.

It will rain as they wake to how I'm not there,
as train-rattle piles through the evening air
that holds my silence and stills my tongue
as our garden fills and swells with its song.

Esperanto Anonyme

My name is Mark and

after Charles Bernstein

I am a northern poet, a northwestern poet,
a northeastern poet, a Stockton poet,
a Preston poet, a Teesside poet,
a domestic poet, a political poet,
an evasive poet, a formal poet, an ex-
perimental poet, a reflective poet, a strategic poet,
a part-time poet, an evenings and weekends poet,
a 24 hour party poet, a performance poet,
a preschool poet, a streetwise poet,
a smart arse poet, a wry poet,
a real poet, a male poet, people's poet,
a blue poet, a red poet, a green poet,
a black-white-and-read-all-over poet,
a ready made poet, a donkey of a poet,
I am a love poet in the morning,
a darkly comic poet over lunch,
a post-prandial second language poet,
a crispy edge of the lasagne poet at teatime,
a pop poet watching the telly,
and an interrogative poet in the sack,
I am a creative poet, a restricted poet,
a poet making the most of slender means,
a listed poet, a candidate poet,
a could-have-been-a-contender poet,
a difficult decision making poet,
a still young poet, a poet with a maturing voice,
a gritty poet, a can-I-take-it-to the-bridge-
yeah-go-on-take-it-to-the-bridge poet,
an anti-poet, a poet who hates beauty
for its own sake and its own good,
a poet after Auschwitz and the poet who
put the ram in the ramalamadingdong,
I am a vernacular poet, a poet
of exquisite juxtapositions,
a poet inhabited by inhibition,

I am a poet with a mission,
a missionary poet with a million positions,
a beat poet, jazz poet, spoken word poet,
I am an ironic poet, a post-punk poet,
a just-add-boiling-water poet,
a poet with attitude, a fraudulent poet,
a situationist poet, a dead poet,
a situation-communist poet,
I am an accessible poet, I am a poet
banging a tambourine, I am a poet with a headache.
backache and an indefinable langour,
a terminal case of ennui,
I am a discursive poet, a generative poet,
an imagist who scorns the sketch,
a poet driven by the need for results,
a leaving poems poet, a birth of your child poet
a research poet, a poet ever puzzled,
a product poet, a process poet,
an executive Top Management Poet,
I am a terraced house poet, a pacifist
terrorist poet with a pillowful of feathers,
an erotic poet, a dream poet, a dream-song-sung-blue poet,
a poet without a home, a poet in his place,
a poet crying for mother and apple pie,
a stir-fried tofu poet, a white bread black pudding poet,
I am a poet in the field, a poet at large,
a systems poet, a computer generated poet,
a small press poet, a hard pressed poet,
a depressed poet, a suppressed poet,
a poet reeling with surprise and delight,
a husband poet, son poet, brother poet,
dad poet, a dadaist poet, a sudden movement poet,
a martian poet, a poet behaving badly,
a talkin-'bout-my-generation poet,
a post-post-post-post-post poet,
a modernist poet in the market place,
a gnomic poet on the street corner,
a never-going-to-be-on-the-South-Bank-Show poet,
a tea-time local news poet, a tense poet,
a speak my weight poet, an eat my words poet,

an educated poet, a philistine poet,
an aesthetic principles don't butter the bread poet,
a poetry boom revival poet, a dusty corner poet,
a shabbier the better poet, an alphabetical order poet,
a dictionary poet, a tip of the tongue poet,
a poet in a mess, a you-hum-it-I'll-play-it poet,
a stop-this-poem-I-want-to-get-off poet.

'And that the world is not joke, nor any part of it a sham'

(Walt Whitman)

this dark this steam this smuggling
this work this heat this wondering
this tooth this brow this bothering
this cap this chip this knuckling
this desk this bone this dithering
this glass this drink this guzzling
this tongue this key this tingling
this light this ear this lathering
this night this name this painting
this itch this ache this ironing
this ridge this fall this rioting
this sigh this vim this visioning
this walk this hearth this heartening
this ache this bed this angering
this quest this zest this zipping
this smile this slip this crumbling
this tic this tack this editing
this joke this door this juddering
this mop this floor this muttering
this knife this orb this offering
this pint this page this dialing
this quid this swag this quivering
this plate this urge this uddering
this hex this switch this exiting
this fudge this grudge this fidgeting
this yell this end this yattering

At the top of the tree keep climbing

beneath the road's metallic song
the solid tenderness of earth
softened bark of a fingertip
running gently down your spine

*

in the bed of leaves the root
in the knot of roots the earth
in the clutch of earth the seed
in the tick of seed the explosion

*

listen to the birds' cries slowly turn
from blue to rust to golden
here is a spade to dig with,
rubble and earth to build with

*

behind you: an invisible forest
a clutch of seeds not quite knee-high
the spit and spoils of struggle
a new map of dappled sunlight

*

names carved into trees and bridges
names and what's been done
all those good intentions
sighs made solid in cold morning air

*

ironstone and leafshade root and grow
work muscles into view then spits
bloodred sootblack nicotine yellow
heiroglyphs on the pavements

*

if a tree is a powerline
a forest is a message in a bottle
and just what the quiet means
the leaves keep to themselves

Ceremony

I

A man walks out into a field looking for a tune to hum.
His overcoat is the colour of his wife's pastry when it's
left a few minutes too long. He's thinking about his daughter
and the dissolute life he fears she lives at University.
The horizon is a blackening of hedgerows behind
his late September shadow. In his pocket he play with stones
he's had since he was thirteen. He reaches the field set aside
to do nothing in and offers up a prayer for his daughter,
starts to bury a small black box of dirt in the fine soil,
breaking the earth with his hands, patting it flat again after.

At his kitchen sink, scrubbing the black earth from beneath his nails,
as his wife proudly lifts from the over a pie without
even a tinge of brown, even around the fluted edges,
he starts to whisper a circular tune that goes on all night.

II

Eighteen, she reverses the car down the long path to the road
without turning her head, plunges backwards into the picture
held in the rear-view mirror, the white gate shining in the dusk.
She swings the car round sending stones skidding into the grass
and then follows her full beam into the dark. A healthy sneer
competes with a smile just beneath the pale surface of her face.
The night and the car combine, an hour she experiences
as a memory even as she moves so swiftly through it.

The town throws its cheap necklace of street lights up to catch
behind its back, places it carefully around her neck
as she accelerates through amber near the iron works.
She is singing along to a record the radio played
a mile back, when she was still alone in the dark, travelling
through her own thoughts, feeling a stranger on these familiar roads.

III

She stands at the kitchen door and watches them go, each
            leaving
some presence around the table, mud from his boots, her
            perfume.
She traces the boundaries of her land, the outside edges
of fields whose neatness is almost an obsession, almost
the only reason he heaves himself from their bed most
            mornings,
while she is up and about setting yeast to bubble and bread
to rise and fill the room with the smell of a contented home.
She looks without affection at the table where she breakfasts
alone, sits down at it and rubs her palms against the grain,
runs a nail down the cracks to remove some drying pastry.

She lowers and turns her head, lays it on her forearms as if
someone was stood behind her rubbing her shoulders with his
            thumbs.
Her hands that had been fists open, her eyes close, she starts to
            dream
while the oven creaks and the rest of the house holds its
            silence.

Documentary

I knew what would happen next.
I walked out backwards into the yard.
There was a huge onion on the step.
It smelt of acrid string and Thatcherism.
I burst into tears and sobbed uncontrollably.
If you'd have asked me why, I'd have said nothing.
I was incoherent and uncomplaining.
How the hell could an onion smell of a political doctrine?
On estates to the north of Stockton they would tell you.
They would open the shutters slightly.
They would put out a fist to meet your nose.
They would explain that there is little difference.
They were used to finding onions on their doorsteps.
I was not, I was downright puzzled into anger by it.
I'd have turned round and wormed my way back in again.
But words cannot be unspoken.
Besides, there was now a chicken on my doorstep.

Faction

If no one's making a documentary
about your struggle with the plumbing
how can you be sure your blisters are real?
The pipe that connects the bath to the outside world
won't bend in quite the way your dogma says it should.

We all know what's going to happen next.
It is time for diplomacy and then coercion
or for the fucking pipe to be introduced
to the pleasures and perversions of the bidet
until the floor is littered with broken porcelain.

Then remorse will flood the room like water.

Gospel

The ist with an itch
to prove god knows what
holds up an aubergine
and begs me check the seeds,
read the message revealed by his knife.

I tell him there are circles and patterns
that salt could draw out,
though no meaning but layers
in brown lentil moussaka,
or a gala production of my bengan bhaji.

He refuses to be disappointed
and points out the limits of my vocabulary.

Reply

*'Now that physics is proving the intelligence of the universe
what are we to do about the stupidity of humankind?'*
(Jeanette Winterson)

Not stupid, just make pictures like rocks do.
Slow and big, not changing, just forgotten,
scratch out mud and dig till done again.
Hard thinker, like muscle and breath mixed
with dirt find under fingernails when gnash stubs.
Dark muscle. Not so dumb as daylight.
Always can turn black. Or red. Always find
hole to hurt with. Is fun.
Bang head on smooth rock. Grip tight.
Not stuck. Know how to add dreams up.
Take away to rub together to make fire.
In orbit round fires and flesh, need nothing
make better, happier. Sleep heavy.
Not stupid, just slow to wake like ice in sun.

If I said I was reading

The Collected Poems of Ted Berrigan
whilst watching *The X Factor*,
having cooked tofu, broccoli and garlic noodles,
with the sake I brought back from Japan,
the morning spent recycling cardboard
and the afternoon at the gym to watch
the football results happen on Sky Sports,
North End throwing away an early lead,
and that I was somehow caught in the bosom
of my family in the warmth of the evening,
would you raise a glass in quiet praise
or reach for my mum's favourite question
to enquire in the most neutral of tones
whether I was bragging or complaining?

Advice

Ideas should not be mistaken for facts
as this can lead to ligament damage.
Put safety to one side, especially
where love and late tackles from behind
are concerned, and remember
Risk Assessment hardens the arteries.

Don't forget the ear is erogenous,
and rain a prophylactic,
but dribble or drool is never attractive.
Grammar doesn't matter, but neither
does it hurt, and sloppy vowel sounds
dilute the ardour of passion.

A hunch is worth more than a theory,
and never needs a bibliography.
Don't wait for please and thank you
and don't get caught watching clouds.
If you want a job doing, dance around it
till it wails for mercy, then leave.

Sincerity breeds indiscretion.
Ladders are useful but should be held
by a big man with his foot on the first rung,
whistling a tune too complex for his lips.
Don't let the ladder actually touch the ground.
It's not true nobody likes a smart arse.

Minutes

The Escape Committee noted the fast car
parked outside, engine running, door open
and the champagne truffles on the dash.
It approved the intention, but raised in discussion
several points of order. It approved the revving
of the engine but withheld commitment
to the foot hitting the floor, fearing excess.
It considered suggestions that future funding
schemes linked to widening provision
might be available to support such projects.

The Standing Committee for Prevarication
has yet to meet.

The Committee for Cross-Faculty Co-operation
and Promotion of the Simple Life received
twelve reports and noted the excellent work.
Following discussion it was agreed that
the distinctive innovative nature of the progress
had been achieved several times before by all present.
It noted the importance of the past being
scrupulously embraced by the future.
The Committee approved a motion for biscuits.

The Standing Committee for Urgent Matters
of Unspecifiable Natures withdrew its minutes.

The Committee for Quality and Standards
noted a worrying decline in the area of coffee,
and highlighted several further areas of weakness
including biscuits, blue biros, light bulb consumption
and the irritating bleeps of the photocopier.
It welcomed a rating of 23 for marker pens.
It condemned the common practice of arranging
chocolate biscuits plain side up, and recommended
that guidelines be established for this and
included in induction of all new staff.

The broadness of certain of the male lecturers' lapels
was noted as a concern which may need to be
looked at in closer detail at some future point.

The Standing Committee for the Establishment
of Priorities hopes to meet within the next month.

The Committee for the Blatantly Obvious
considered suggestions that everything
had been perfectly predictable and that members
has in fact been warned. It confirmed that
it had, indeed, told them so. It received, noted
and denied accusations of having set a precedent
by painting over windows, taping up doors
and the establishment of road blocks.
It approved overwhelmingly a vote for
the continuation of the work of the Committee
under a new title of Committee for Common Sense.

The Standing Committee for Next Steps
has been postponed indefinitely.

By rote

remember the new deal
       the new coke
              the new diet coke
remember the new boom
       the new bust
              the new franchise
remember the new love
       the new free love
              the new sobriety
remember the new drugs
       the new drink
              the new escapism
remember the new society
       the new permissive society
              the new wistfulness
remember the new fruit
       the new yoghurt
              the new jive
remember the new fifties
       the new jazz
              the new funk
remember the new depression
       the new war
              the new nostalgia
remember the new tradition
       the new innovation
              the new forgetting
remember the new message
       the new instant message
              the new noodle
remember the new literacy
       the new book
              the new blank sheet
remember the new author
       the new death of the author
              the new broom

remember the new pop
        the new revival
                the new new revival
remember the new avant-pop
        the new avant-garde
                the new old guard
remember the new yesterday
        the new tomorrow
                the new moment
remember the new up-lighting
        the new shadows
                the new seekers
remember the new ice
        the new breakfast
                the new tv
remember the new boom
        the new bust
                the new marketing
remember the new look
        the new morality
                the new decadence
remember the new thought
        the new ignorance
                the new man
remember the new lad
        the new ladette
                the new sex
remember the new vernacular
        the new glamour
                the new comedy
remember the new excess
        the new psychiatry
                the new faith
remember the new beat
        the new beatles
                the new times
remember the new youth
        the new parents
                the new lyric

remember the new chic
      the new heroin chic
            the new cinema
remember the new sixties
      the new seventies
            the new proles
remember the new technology
      the new classlessness
            the new beauty
remember the new insomnia
      the new amnesia
            the new workplace
remember the new distraction
      the new displacement
            the new discipline
remember the new virgins
      the new flares
            the new popular front
remember the new angst
      the new psychedelia
            the new psychedeliasmith
remember the new situation
      the new partnership
            the new greed
remember the new information
      the new criticism
            the new excuse
remember the new witchhunt
      the new audience
            the new intellectuals
remember the new punk
      the new wave
            the new new wave of new punk
remember the new school
      the new old school
            the new old school tie
remember the new style
      the new black
            the new retro

remember the new acid
the new net
the new world
remember the new left
the new right
the new muddle
remember the new relationship
the new infidelity
the new sainthood
remember the new commerce
the new e-commerce
the new shopping
remember the new consumer
the new comment
the new shoes
remember the new city
the new country
the new crime
remember the new shape
the new tight
the new silhouette
remember the new loft
the new cuisine
the new garnish
remember the new mod
the new neo-mod
the new post-neo-mod
remember the new fatherhood
the new pottery
the new biodiversity
remember the new fusion
the new novel
the new epic
remember the new neighbourhood
the new community
the new masses
remember the new education
the new science
the new culture

remember the new change
        the new hope
                the new failure
remember the new terror
        the new green
                the new clampdown
remember the new space
        the new generation
                the new next generation
remember the new dance
        the new regionalism
                the new fame
remember the new dirt
        the new centre
                the new opportunities
remember the new empowerment
        the new hard times
                the new day
remember new reality
        the new face
                the new unacceptable face
remember the new news
        the new newspeak
                the new now

Song of the man with a glass half-full

for Andy Croft

I think it's time I had a word
about some territories absurd,
of heaven, happiness and hell,
and other places prone to swell
with watery confusion.

I'm not an easy man to please.
I don't go down on bended knees.
I don't take kindly to defeat,
don't find that 'nearly' tastes as sweet
as victory's retribution.

The morning says the world's a mess,
the afternoon agrees and, yes,
we could cry over milk that's spilt,
let broken axes spin or tilt,
but that is no solution.

I think the glass may be half-full.
I don't think that that makes me dull.
I'd rather praise the bit we've got
than concentrate on what we've not
brought home to resolution.

Romantic gloom may keep us pure.
The undone act's the most secure.
But choice can make a little change,
more than the deckchairs rearrange
to help our dissolution.

Though far from ideal our results
will ignore empty small insults
of those who want it all right now
but never manage to say how
they'll make their contribution.

So step by step, and drink by drink,
we'll show the world a way to think -
half-glasses raised to toast the health
of an optimistic commonwealth
that's built on imperfection.

Tender openings

Two sentences for Lester Bowie

1.
Because I have written that poem before
and the couscous needs steaming, let us
abandon the last two hours, and given that
the heat's curlicues have woven their italics
round the melting watering cans that chew
and spit out each morsel of the dusk,
let us attempt some scruffy ordered thing
to accompany this red and green dance
that makes the tip of the tongue tingle
with a precious name simply out of reach.

2.
Lonely man blows down a blue banana,
whistles himself a scratchy hello
fast firm and pouting to last,
goes sinuous through toxic dreams
latin-edged in longing's girth and grit,
finito for God's bent mirage
but roped tight to that tired true woman,

a woman tried until innocent of hope,
miracle tender in her hot-danced finish,
grit no more an issue than let-me-in,
dreams of sky open for comings and goings,
lasting and endurance of the slow, the slow, the fast
hello and goodbye as blood worms away, whistles
banana-ed blue and bruised and blowing so lonely.

Exhalation for a singer

The breaths she took were massive,
and the change she made was deep.
The air she trapped and then let go
by war then peace then war was shaped
to meet this world's numb cold full on,
to take offence and make defiant
sympathy with simple pain.
She was not going to stand for it.

In the darkness there would be flowers
and in the silence there would be song,
for a tune is like a long, long life,
born in the air, but made in the lungs.
The world she made was massive,
and the breaths she took were deep.

The contemporary anecdote

Success links sleight of hand
To coy looks and bristling hairs.
All his life he found engagement
Parties and other social collisions
Just so many unreasonable demands.
Indeed, when that simplistic performer
Lust showed its un-English face,
He retraced his steps and leant on the bar,
Wishing it would turn into the counter
Of the Popeye's New Horizons chippy.
Evening against the walls and shutters
Was pink and blue and hopeful,
And the bouncers' conversation turned
To plums and which was the sweeter,
The Victoria or the Elephant Heart,
And how the French Damson was best
for jam, complete with boiled stones.
This was all the encouragement needed
For an ambush of his good intentions
And the founding of the Drunken School
Of Paradox, its inaugural lecture flowing
From the stool on the end of the bar,
Down Armitage's marble telephone,
And finally and most spectacularly,
From the requisitioned microphone
Of the pub singer, desperate to get away.
The most lamentable phrase never arrived,
Though we could all see it bubbling,
Contempt defining its own versatility,
Playing on his lips like a tune.
The moon recurs and a man on a bike
Looks down at him sitting on the pavement.
Tradition is nothing if not regular,
He mutters to himself, glancing back at the lights,
Language is nowt if not oppressive.
Fate draws endlessly on its truisms.
This landscape is literal and cadenced,
Deafeningly mistaken and always hungover.

On making

a response to Albert Goldbarth's 'Beauty', for rednile

Readying himself for work – the sky just blue enough
to confront the dark with its clear diction –
his cramped chest felt him crudely dream
through ragged, bubbling rememberings: electric
balloons, paperbag heads, dazed action paintings
stacked on the racks of a tin-shed warehouse.
Each work a future hard to tell from daybreak.
Breakfast spoke over the dream and the art
with its flattening drone, and his idea was cornered,
cowered there while he sang that dream in one of his
many pirouetting tunes. The pillow's buttoned mind
that once protested so vigorously – every night,
over every scrap of salt – shuttered now.

But still he rolls his sleeves, pushes open the door
and frets not over order, nor fears the morning.
Who is money to suggest that making does not turn this earth?

When aid is no help

That is not a solution,
that is a sausage on a stick.
The quizmaster misunderstands
paraphrased seduction.
The lights go out.
You have won the booby prize,
the darkened room awaits,
needle clicks in the eternal present.
Life / death is a spondee
split by our stuttering.
Neither Anish Kapoor
nor IKEA
can save you now.

13 ways of looking at Tony

1
Half a dozen dull shadows
on the Sunday tea-time news
and the only shining thing
was Tony's smile in its weekend chair
trying to convince itself
it really existed.

2
The 7.10 direct to King's Cross
and the latest daring revision,
mentioned casually in the papers,
made my heart tired and bowed, like a tree
in which are posted three photos of Tony
and his family.

3
Tony stood firm, inscrutable and therefore inspiring.
It was the leading role in the Autumn pantomime.

4
A man and a woman
Are one.
A man and a woman and Tony
Are a Policy Review.

5
I'm not sure which is worse:
the wind rustling through the emptiness of the words
or the beauty of the fudge that becomes a kind of smut,
Tony in mid-speech,
or the applause just after.

6
In the name of an indecipherable cause,
we go along with Tony, the idea
of the necessity of him.
Icicles bar the window and we would censure
the sun that dared to suggest melting them.

7
Hey, you, thin youths of the North East,
why steal the golden cars and dream of speed?
Can you not see Tony there by the roadside,
sticking out his thumb?

8
I can tell a dream when I have one,
have sussed the pragmatism of the saints even,
but I know when I am being told to keep shtum.
I know that Tony is implicated
in this scary knowledge.

9
When Tony is not on tv,
he lets us know the outer limits
of what his counterpart *The Lion King*
called the Circle of Life, lets us see
the grubby fingers of the animator.

10
At the sight of Tony
behind the quasi-invisible autocues
raising his voice just a little,
not too much,
even the leader writers must
wither slightly somewhere inside.

11
He rides through Sedgefield
in his Austin Allegro,
mistaking the empty road in the rear view
for Tony about to flash him
and gesture for him to slow down.

12
The river is flowing on the other side of the park.
Looking at it earlier this lazy Sunday, the kids
saw a dog they decided thought it was a fish,
because it was swimming.
This has nothing to do with Tony.

13
All afternoon I have been waiting
for an explanation of this stiffness down
my left side, this cramp rattling my chest.
I have examined my life and decided
it must be down to Tony,
the giving-in his shape stands for.
This is doubtless unfair.

1995

In the tent

'Notorious for conducting his business meetings in tents,
Gaddafi travels with one everywhere he goes.'
(Time)

Be careful whose tent you enter.
You may find yourself smiling at things
that would suck water from deserts.
You may find yourself breathless
and wishing for a wind beyond the canvas.
The tent is a bubble, remember.
In the tent it is warm. There are cakes
and drinks that take all edges off.
The air is rich and sweetly perfumed.
The desert never ends, takes water where it can.
It is neutral and gets everywhere, the sand.

You cannot control who comes into the tent.
You cannot shape them to your wishes.
Remember this: the tent is not neutral.
It takes over any space you care to pitch it in.
It is not a vacuum, but dark matter.
What is in the tent is what's missing.
There is nothing in the tent
but it makes the weight of the world.
It shapes and carves and kills
with unfathomable design,
so simple, so elegant a solution.

It makes you invisible, but your silhouette
will be magnified and projected.
We can see you. We know you are
no longer awkward inside the tent.
We know you are smiling, know how you
excuse yourself when nature calls,
shuffle away like the breathless scorpion,
unembarrassed by our hate.

But we know you are in there,
and we will wait.

For the Immigration Minister on the occasion of his birthday

with apologies to Thomas Lynch
and for more than one Minister

May I open by saying how very much
you are on my mind, how rare it is
I forget about your precious contribution
to the safety and moral welfare of our home.
I hope today finds you wearing your best smile,
the one put aside for tight by-elections.
Be sure that if a series of virulent and pus-flooding
cold sores were to spread determinedly
from the edges of that warm tough-love smile to
the edges of your face I would not be glad,
would not clap my hands together
and break out into a spontaneous scat frenzy.

Neither would it gladden my weary heart
to see you dragged away and summarily tried
for some grotesque sex crime involving
kittens, sellotape, a public highway
and a piping bag full of whipped cream.
And if your nationally broadcast alibi
was ignored by the bent and paid-off jury
I would consider it an indictment
of society that such a thing could happen
to such a fine example of humanity.
The thought of what the kitchen boys
would kindly add to your prison porridge
would give not the slightest satisfaction,
I am proud to be able to say.

I sincerely hope - no, pray - that news
does not reach me that your wife has been
carried off by Revivalist Militants
to a secret camp finally found only
when the high-pitched revelry
she introduces to their rather dour culture
grows too much for the neighbours,
who reluctantly call in the SAS.
That your wife takes five of them out
before surrendering and being dragged
kicking, screaming, and with an impressive
rendition of the Internationale
dashing from her lips would only cause
greater, deeper sympathy to flow
from my already gushing heart.
I can only express my hope that she settle
and return to the normal life she was once
lucky enough to enjoy under your care.

May your birthday bring you luck:
may it not lead to walking the bottom
of Lake Windermere in concrete boots,
the victim of an unusually ruthless
and effective cabinet reshuffle.
May the packages you open not be bombs
left by guards with dubious taste in jokes.
May you enjoy your breakfast
free of the attentions of pubic lice,
infestations of cockroaches, gnats,
wasps, bees, or fleas so numerous
you mistake them for black sesame seeds.

I bear you no grudges, and have no envy
of the difficult - some would say impossible -
task you have set to with so much vigour.
Long may you avoid the ravages Tourette's
Syndrome would wreak on your oratory.
Let us see this coming year as an opportunity
to lay aside all the minor shortcomings
that have helped to make you so important
to so many people: without your quirks,
you would not be so lovable though
- so don't go changing.

The first person I hear today who calls you
a beast-loving cod-breathed deranged
excuse for a free-loading gowk with a hump
intoning jism and kindergarten lies,
mean, nihilistic, a pervert queasy
from ringworm, subviral, tedious,
unlikely to verbalise anything other than waffle,
or a xenophobe yabbering zeugma after zeugma
will, rest assured, feel the full force of my anger.

Variations on William Carlos Williams, 'for' Kosovo, originally

I'm sorry, I have eaten the stones you fought so fiercely for.
They smelt so much like bread
and were so filling. You will find more.

**

I'm sorry, we have cut off the water supply.
You will be better off without it.
It would only have reminded you.

**

I'm sorry, we have murdered your mother,
father, husband, three of your four sons and your daughter.
They are in a better place.

**

I'm sorry, we have burnt out your house.
The flames looked beautiful against the dark sky,
and the few bricks standing have a kind of grandeur.

**

I'm sorry, we have allocated your territory
to someone who will use it better.
It was never what you needed, or wanted really.

**

I'm sorry, the pictures on your walls
have been translated into ashes. They were cheap,
and never really gave the impression you hoped.

**

I'm sorry you have to go. It was probably time.
The morning was so fresh and new,
and the neighbourhood not what it was.

**

I'm sorry, we have decided to give you your freedom.
You will enjoy it, it is so sweet and precious,
and lasts longer than a single lifetime.

Words for a minute's silence

Let the broad shoulders
of this still afternoon
take the dead weight
of a beaker of tears.
Plait ropes from sand
to pile at the scene
till the wind blows them
into tight averted eyes.
Go home by Weeping Cross.
Consult the book of platitudes.
With the millstones your tears
turn to as they fall
grind the light from daisies,
the hope from buttercups,
the colour from the hot-house
blooms of other people's Spring,
and use all that to start again.

A new guide to Seaton Carew

after Kenneth Koch

'The attendant in charge of this toilet is not responsible for articles left in this convenience'

1.
Look at this café. It is open.
The sign outside says so, though it is smirking
when it says it, and leaning back on its heels
pretending it is Jean Gabin, hiding away
in grainy sea-fretted days.
If this place had a hat, it would be pulled
low over the forehead. It would be
black, and greasy on the inside.

2.
Look at these coins. They fall from light
with a clatter like hooves on a street
a hundred years ago, like rocks feeling it
as they slowly turn to sand.
They want the darkness of a pocket,
but are thrust back into the waterfall
of small change that recycles itself,
always just one more to make everything
tumble, endlessly, endlessly, endlessly.

3.
Look at this rain. The Nichols Family
have the Latest British and American Amusements,
but we have the rain, cake walking
down the prom in high dudgeon,
hissing gossip into the doorways
of shops that may not open next summer.
This rain has the disordered personality
of a man who talks to strangers at bus stops.
It is wholly innocent, but frightening.
It may never stop.

4.
Look at this dog. It runs along the beach
in a frenzy of matted hair, mongrel bitch
of the Café Royal and the Golf Course.
The sea is trying to catch it, to pull it in,
but it can't reach. If it could reach a dog,
could it bear to forgo the town?
The sea is endlessly disappointed
with its position and its place.

5.
Look at this clock. And these bus stops.
And the toilets. The white deco curves
lean into another time, another place.
It was made out of love, like the Taj Mahal,
and it remains out of stubbornness.
It will not give up being beautiful
just to satisfy our pitiful expectations.
Go away and be happy, it whispers in your ear
as you stride urgently towards the toilets.

6.
Look at the man waiting for his bus,
a single grey scratch against the stone,
like something someone forgot to pick up
when their bus arrived, late again.
This is not a place you can wait only
for a bus back to Hartlepool.
To the south, where the landscape
turns alien to provide for us,
where earth is more metal than dirt,
and lights pattern themselves
through and beyond abstraction,
the wrong switch flicked in tiredness
could blacken the land and welcome the sea.
This man is not worrying about that.
He wants to know where his bus is.
He thinks he is still waiting for a bus.

Basho visits the Headland, Hartlepool

smell of frying bacon
　　　　the dew still meshing into string vests over the
　　　　　　dawn's beergut
flat dregs of stout veil the bottom of the glass

*

quoits of light on the virtual nets
　　　　ion-thin splash of white-haired water
how much is the entrance fee?

*

seagulls knot around angled spires
　　　　drunken fishwet night
startled freshness of stone

*

just a triple jump to the slag-carved gare
　　　　a skimmed stone's grace away
firefly slashes of molten steel

*

sea or third division roar
　　　　shell bound ear and swelling strings
to move on up or move on out

*

religious glitter of the shopping mall
　　　　a sigh in a sheltered ear
chill hair's attention along a frightened spine

*

take my leave into the blind fret
　　　　the thin skyline stuttering eternity
thigh high in cold stabbing sea

How to make revolutions

Two museums on the same block show
Frieda Kahlo and Diego Rivera had more
of an eye for interior décor than their neighbour
Trotsky. Their house sunnier blue
and deeper yellow than we can dream now
burst with making, with rescued shape.
Trotsky never even filled in the bullet holes,
Siqiueros' most extreme mural, left them there
to see the last three months of his struggle.
(An artist assassin! It took a businessman to succeed.)
Trotsky's bookcases are neat, the Kahlo house
seeming chaos, box files of political notes
rub up against 'From Here To Eternity'.
Burt Lancaster and Deborah Kerr in the waves
they were not, and I imagine Trotsky went round for
            his tea
more often than they came to him, but I feel
them all laughing in hope and anger,
returning to their studios, to clay, to oils,
to papier-maché, to face, thread, plot, fruit.

On not going to Liverton Mines to find a girl seen on a bus

Ô toi que j'eusse aimée, ô toi qui le savais!
Baudelaire

It's not such a hard decision to make,
this bus back to Liverton Mines
or watching the sky tie knots in the gloom
to help it remember this town.
But she doesn't look pleased, has a face to split rocks,
a gob to spit out bones.

It could be the smell, though that's not reached the peak
by now that it will have tonight,
when drunks wobble off and put their heads down
for the chippy at the end of the street,
none of them giving a pit pony's piss
about the wisdom of the comfort of fat.

Or it could be the engine's dull mimicking whine,
or the tempting emergency door
right at the back she was taught to avoid
on endless trips out with her mother.
But it probably isn't. It's sweet nothing to do
with Liverton Mines or anyone, anything, there

and all to do with anywhere, everywhere else.
But she wouldn't tell you, that much is plain,
the way her eyes see beyond hills to the sea.
So let her ride that bus. Keep walking, knock down
that drink you want to make your eyes sting.
Forget about ever going to Liverton Mines.

Annaghmakerig Kelpie

*A kelpie is a water spirit said to lure travellers to
their deaths*

Bellies full but wanting inspiration
to clear their heads of spirits marshaling
words or colours into striking line
they come down from The Big House.
The water stays where the lake sets it,
though the rain makes it swell, and the wind
crinkles it to crêpe, silvered by the moon.
I move inside the lapping near their sensitive
feet and slap against stones like tentative
applause, from an uncertain audience.
Sometimes I'll pick the windiest of these blow-ins
and when the clouds close in and damp tightens
to the first signs of rain I'll take the shape
of a dog or even, for the more romantic,
a deer, and follow them up and through the gorse,
only ever half-appearing, turning
my shy face to their inquisitive eyes
as they turn and wonder, wander round the mud
they don't dare get on their shoes, and up again
to The Big House where I'll shift into the cat
to bother them for bacon rind or a sniff
of chamomile or a peek in the dictionary.
Spooked by they don't know what, they wait
anxiously, eagerly, to empty the dishwasher.
I slip back into the lake and sing to the moon
of my unique benevolence.

After buying John Tranters' *Urban Myths* in the Australian Experimental Art Foundation bookshop, Adelaide, I decide not to take the tram to Glenelg as advised but to write a pantoum in homage instead

I shall, I think, avoid the beach:
This pale and aging carapace
Is not the kind that's fit to share
With young folk revelling bronze.

This pale and aging carapace
Would read John Tranter's sly pantoums
With young folk revelling bronze
Around, about and over-egged,

Who'd read John Tranter's sly pantoums
As something odd for by the water,
Around, about and over-egged
in graceful waves, unlike my English sweat.

Someone odd down by the water,
They'd say of me, eyebrows vaulted
In graceful waves, unlike my English sweat
That sits and glows, and pinkly glowers.

They'd say of me, eyebrows vaulted,
I'd thrust on the day a literary bent,
That sits and glows and pinkly glowers
its own peace, keeps a quiet belligerence.

I'd thrust upon the day a literary bent,
Were I to feel the breeze a-whistling
Its piece, attuned to quiet belligerence.
Best to keep things within my head.

Were I to feel a breeze a-whistling
It'd not be the kind that's fit to share.
Best to keep things within my head:
I shall, I think, avoid the beach.

Frome Street Monologue

And I am purposeful about that, actually
she said to him quite calmly
not using the word as she would in a meeting
but as if talking of something intimate
to be said tonight or not at all:

here in the Adelaide evening heat
exactly as I walk past
leaving him no right of reply.

Another, further, variation on Du Fu

for Sonwabo Meyi

Like mountain walkers in the mist,
people's lives pass each other by,
the chance for stories lost.

Where did I come from and why,
your daughter asks, not unwelcoming,
just keen to know, wide eyed, bright.

I stood back from my world to come here,
sought to change the season
to see my aging face and place afresh.

We share the candle-light of words,
swap places like swallows do not.
In both homes we are the same bird.

Tomorrow mountains and seasons
and the world's business will separate us.
What distance makes invisible

art's memory makes distinct.

Imagine a city

Imagine a city where now it is winter.
Seven bridges blink at the cold iron light.
The coal sleeps soundly, miles down, as the sea
Does its damnedest to chorus the angels awake.
But what use this song, what use this song?

Dark Queen Victoria ponders her masses.
Stag dos and hen nights burn down their huts.
A quick dance, a last chance, part of our dreaming:
The staggering youth in luxurious loss.
But what use this song, what use this song?

Now imagine a city where us sun-shy Bessies
Get in the van and drive to the hills.
Houses scattered like cold blue trumpet notes
Grow from the earth and take to the road.
What use this song, what use this song?

The wild coast between here and there, now
And then is not so solid, can melt into air.
But in Gateshead or Craddock we live as we breath,
Sharing the air with each other and angels.
What use this song, what use this song?

Imagine a city loud with their laughter
As hate after hate slides into the surf.
Are we so blind that we still cannot see
Like cattle our dreams line up, undeferred?
What use this song, what use this song?

Imagine a city where the angels watch
Our mothers and fathers dance in our dreams.
Would it not be a place of light, with so much
Forgiveness, so much hope just about to be?
What use this song, what use this song?

And what use would angels be, if the wind were
Still bitter through so many sighs and sobs?
The location our dreams, our ancestors sing us
Back to calm, on into the unknown.
What use this song, what use this song?

That melody grows like an elephant's ears,
Tumbles over its playmates, a new memory
That catches the banks and climbs ashore.
Connect the head to the hips to the brain to the heart.
What use this song, what use this song?

When our bridges stretch they reach all the way here,
Where to heal is not treason and song is a promise.
Some things it takes an angel to forgive.
And angels cross worlds with their tunes.
What use this song, what use this song?

So imagine a city in two places at once.
Its people are sweating, for their work is hard.
They are making the future by the light of the past
And the angels are smiling, smiling at last.
What use this song, what use this song?

Port Elizabeth, Eastern Cape, 2007

Home as a cornucopia

Makers of pastry and shapers of pies,
builders of houses and mortgage providers,
bankers, crafters, tanker-drivers, shops,
counters of beans and makers of scenes,
conjurers of light and houses from hats,
creators of mats, offices, homes,
scaffolders, miners, benders, combiners,
those who run trains and boats and planes
 – and cars, vans, bikes, trucks and lorries,
frothers up of headlines and local stories,
potash, iron, marshmallows, paninis, cakes,
country houses, open mines and mucky works,
people who pluck pictures from the air to make
photos, blueprints, fresh-baked pizzas, songs,
the people who give you ice creams,
toffees, tarmac, sleep-filled nights, insurance,
sharpeners of pencils, bakers of bread,
the ports, the malls, and the roads up to them,
the fillers of airways, airwaves and glasses,
pullers of pints and molten steel, lager and bitter
and mild mannered curries, mixers of spices,
pickers of pickles and peppers, proud paper-peddlers,
fryers of fish and chips, trainers of the fat,
blenders of soup and fine tailors of suits,
mixers of cement to fill high heels and boots,
lickers of stamps and blowers of glass,
builders of containers, cisterns and fountains,
breakers of brown-fields, diggers of the dirt,
kickers of footballs, halo-headed chefs,
binders and sellers and printers of books, plain cooks,
cutters of concrete and layers of turf, geniuses
who argue the elements into medicine and art,
lines of melody, memory and meaning,
words, pixels, frames, wash, water, light,
muscles, shape, music, movement, laughter, bite.

from A Balkan Exchange (2007)

Esperanto Anonyme

for Bill Herbert, il lista-creatore migliore

Esperanto na billiardo
Esperanto de statistico
Esperanto of CNN
Esperanto of Chelski and Arsenal
Esperanto ah morning coughs
Esperanto of showerheads
Esperanto da breakfast buffet
Esperanto di bus
Esperanto of football stadia
Esperanto ye barking dogs
Esperanto a empty buzzwords
Esperanto na dead paradigms
Esperanto o't smoking gun
Esperanto of silence
Esperanto di iambs
Esperanto na ragged dance
Esperanto von fear
Esperanto o panic
Esperanto da drum and basics
Esperanto a hips
Esperanto na breath
Esperanto di grafiti
Esperanto de puzzled brows
Esperanto na hope
Esperanto ov hope over experience
Esperanto of beer
Esperanto of lists

Botev v Locomotiv, March 2005,
with added helicopters

Where the teams are named
for poets and revolutionaries
helicopters have been known
to spray rose water onto pitches.
In a hotel guarded by Porsche 4x4s
I saw the Plovdiv derby
turn into a riot with one push.
The keeper let slip his straight red fate,
would not depart, the fans
and his teammates in an argument
that grew like evening rain.
The fat little ref was simply lost,
did not know what he was doing,
rubble showered the touchline.
In the centre circle all he could do
was twist the red and white band
on his wrist, neutral between yellow
and black and white, wonder
what he had done to offend
Grandma Baba Marta
halfway up the terrace,
a rock in her hand, singing
something rude about his father
until the helicopters arrived.

1300 Monument Sofia

So that it can rain Sofia turns inside out,
matt grey, nap smooth, flush with threat.
The fog has lifted, murk revealing dark.

The cast iron rifles of old Russian heroes
are falling bit by slow bit to the ground,
to lie at the foot of this gun-metal mountain

as the taggers of Levski ascend to immortality.
They have new poetry to make that's beyond
the old women marching trolleys across the square

after arm-crossed days in tiny shops
watching the stock gather silent dust.
All that patient mustiness flips the city right.

It is going to rain, and so that it can,
things are going to have to stay like this a while.

Re-entry Blues

On returning to work at Arts Council England after a
week of performances in Sofia, October 2003

When I woke up this morning I was feeling no pain
But I drove me to Darlo and got on the train
I headed for London and as I drew near
I thought 'bout the time that I'd had in Sofia

Got the walking talking
Corporate bend blues

I don't know what I'm doing but I do what I gotta
Just like in rehearsals way up Mount Vitosha
Where Bluba Lu jammed and we poets studied rhyme
And something came out under pressure of time

But now I got the walking talking
Suited booted
Corporate bend blues

I'm a profit agnostic and don't give a damn
But half the North East thinks that I am The Man
Who makes arts decisions and dishes out dough
Though deep in the Balkans they know it's not so

I got the walking talking
Suited booted
Jargon-busting
Corporate bend blues

Now this is a really exceptional meeting
To iambs and pulses my head is still beating
The train speeding there rattles Sofia away
And gives me three hours to think what to say

I got the walking talking
Suited booted
Jargon-busting
Arts transforming
Corporate bend blues

I could be sticking words to beats somewhere near Boyana
Instead I'm playing jargon bingo eating a banana
All I needs a mention of building my capacity
And someone here will get to taste my vigourous tenacity
For making words jump and dance around the table
Seven days of Bulgar blues tell me that I'm able
To pull it out the bag and fill the air with lines
But while meetings are a drag they also feel like mine

So I take the damned tube all the way back to Kings Cross
Kidding myself bout the gain and the loss
A small step forward, not one great leap
By Newark North Gate I am sound asleep

I got the walking talking
Suited booted
Jargon-busting
Arts transforming
Double meaning
Plain English speaking
Corporate bend blues

When the bees are gathering honey

Zig Zag Trio

1.
When the bees are gathering honey
a clarinet will tipsy over the brow
chased by an accordion. It will angle
through the undergrowth till it taps
blunt nose against rock.
It will spiral vexed over screes
of goatskin and whittling wood,
throw dirt behind its back.
Dazed, it will cramp suddenly
when it sees the sunlight,
flitter knuckled song to heavens
it squints to deeper hues
so that it can finally breath again.
It will make its way into the open
and wait for us to form lines around it.
It will tell us they should be circles.

2.
Downstairs, neat young men see us right
for crazy wedding jazz, downstairs
and left into a Cyrillic photograph
where you listen with your eyes, not your hands.
They will describe anything to you,
they say. It is better that way.
I think this is about saving yourself
for a wedding night which may not come.

3.
When I have finished dancing
I will hang a sheet from the window,
covered in honey and rose water.
Then I will wait for the cowbells.

from Half A Mind (1998)

Bringing Down The Government
(Prologue – 1984)

'I've been loving you since the miners' strike…'
Soho

By the time this house has a sea view, and we only
visit the park to recall the kids' paper boats
floating off like illustrations of the wind,
the moment for declarations of love will have passed,
be merely a reference to right now, a shorthand way
to explain lives grown somehow unusual.

We will do nothing all day but sit and wait
for richer friends to return from trips abroad.
Struggle and passion will be nostalgia. The meetings
we snuck out of will be forgotten. It will be like
breathing in and never feeling the breeze behind your rib cage.
It will be as dull as a Sunday spent on a bus.

If we could stop now to pinch the atmosphere
with these urgent fingers, we'd know something
was out of control. It feels like a harmonica solo
swerving past logical limits. It feels like steam in a kettle.
The seas are rising, we don't much care, and nothing
is going to be the same again. Know what? – I love you.

The seas are rising. The summer has blistered my nose
in a new way this year, and that's only the beginning.
The times are decadent and oblivious – it's either funny
or something beyond that, that hurts. What we're most
concerned with is spending more time together,
bringing down the government, and learning to stop smirking.

Know what? I love you. Come
lean on me and watch us stop the future and its tide.
In the distance, if we can take our eyes off each other
for a second, you will see some glowing horizon.
That's where we're headed. That's the big plan.
What we do, what we do with it, is down to us.

I want to work something out:

the realist chaos of the market place,
its tired mugs and hawkers,
the lines, curves, noises and lights
struggling to mean something, a phrase
wheezed out, out of energy, a sham
of a shadow of a mockery of a sham,

has that anything to do with the engine
running beneath my window
and the marks left on the road tomorrow,
the barking that could be a child
hyperventilating through the unspeakable,
if it was not outside where the dog always barks?

I want to work something out.
I don't like to let the sun go down
on a dead end that means mayhem in my dreams.
No one hears my outsized collection
of sardonic jokes when I air them.
I'm glad. I can feel my mouth opening

and closing and the world just carry on.
I want to work something out.
Why I am stood over here when I want
to be over there in a heap with them.
Why I have started overusing the sound I.
Why I don't just shut the fuck up.

This is a travesty of a mockery of a sham.
This is the bottom of the hill
where the cheap light from the high street
ends its search, desperately squawking
as it corkscrews its frantic circles:
'What's the Big Idea? What's the Big Idea?'

As I pack the last of the LPs

the fractious excitement of the unknown
unfolds before us like the A19 in the dark:
you only know it's there when the light shines on it.
This is the grown-up move, where we learn
how much junk we've got we daren't throw away.

We sit among the boxes and the pictures stacked
like so many slices of bread, drink
the last gin, remember when we'd just arrived,
wondering what we will leave behind
for the next couple to exorcise.

In the kitchen there's the smell of garlic
and the dents in the wall where once,
tightening the cupboard doors back on,
I drew blood with the screwdriver,
nearly broke my hand hammering the wall.

The bedroom's bare boards echo, and oddly
it's the time spent ill in bed with chickenpox
that seems to have lingered beneath the rugs,
not the nights we conceived the children,
or the patient painful first times after.

If we've done things wrong here, we forgive ourselves.
When you shut the door and pop the keys through,
all the hours and events we thought were as solid
as my forehead are proved to be dreams
of other lives we might once have led:

we take a last peep through the blinds
we know they hate and expect to see
ourselves moving about, making tea,
putting on a record, making love,
like clips in an ad for a new film, about us.

Today the sky is flat

but you are not, you are almost perfect,
part the air as you walk to leave a calm
following like the wake and gulls behind a ferry.

But from behind your back you produce the pan
I burnt the aduki beans in, tender
bean-shaped holes stippling its black bottom.

I'm always getting things wrong: the world
is full of things struggling to be metaphors
for the exact opposite of everything I dream of.

Sometimes I think I only do this to encourage
the world to be other than it is.
I keep on looking at things as if I imagined them.

I'm trying to stop. I'm sorry about the pan.
In the poem I was writing it was full of water.
It was only just starting to boil.

Song 1

A whiskey & water
a gin on the rocks
a vodka & orange
a rum & black
a fistful of aspirin
for the morning –
and one for yourself.

A Bacardi & coke
a brandy & soda
three fingers of bourbon
a tequila slammer
a foolproof disclaimer
for the morning –
and one for yourself.

A hemlock shandy
a strychnine spritzer
a turps & Tizer
a paraquat & Perrier
and a poultice
for my saintly fevered brow –
and one for yourself.

On the beach near Kinvarra our babies

play on the slate-grey sand.
The football rebounds from the surf
again and again. And again
the spite-sapping wind carries it back,
gently back to our son's excited arms.

I try to clamber out into the foam
along the ragged teeth of the rocks,
but the sand sucks at my unsuitable shoes,
like in Lou's favourite bedtime story
of my escape from building site mud.

You can't stop laughing, keep repeating
'Typical, just exactly typical.'
The sun goes down and turns
the woman gathering Lucky Stones
into a shadow who waves goodbye.

The children chase each other up the slope
to where the seaweed meets the tarmac.
As we negotiate the tortuous roads
to this fortnight's home, they sleep.
We talk of your plans for the garden.

Something pretty. Something indestructible.
The sea returns the ball we left behind.
It rolls down through the weed, floats back.
Rolls down again, is pushed stubbornly back,
until it stays where it has been put.

An April morning gathers itself

the way you straighten your shirt and walk down
to the kitchen. Your bowl chimes against the nail
holding the leaf of the table together.
The mist that was hiding the school playground
clears and the brightness of the day starts to hum
like the rim of a glass under a graceful finger.

The children and I walk the idea of fun
from one end of the park to the other
but it never quite learns to run on its own.
Back home we kick a ball around the garden
to stay out of your way but my mind's set
on other things and I can see you fidgeting.

It feels like weeks since yesterday,
the resolutions, intentions and gin,
the sofa supporting us in whatever we did,
the stairgate coming off right that very minute –
feels like the door we timidly opened is swinging
slowly but surely back in our surprised faces.

By dinnertime the sun is swollen and fierce,
high enough to look down on our compromise.
We think too much about things, we agree,
or not enough, or just the right amount but badly.
The floor we polished before the kids woke up
gets covered with beans that glow in the sunlight.

Song II

Two empty crisp packets
(Worcester Sauce)
A Batman bearing *Good News*
From Readers Digest!
Dog hairs even though
we don't have a dog

A toy fire engine
painted muddy brown
Some long-lost toe nails,
the scissors
Fag ends even though
neither of us smoke

The pink and bitten lid
from the rabbit cup
A knife, a spoon,
a plate and a fork
A sausage roll even though
we don't eat meat

A small attempt
at civilization
developed under
a very low ceiling
Utopias even though
we have taken to pragmatism

Drinking alone in a pub in Bamber Bridge

something, perhaps the jukebox, reminds you
there is a promised land, and it looks like this,
but this is not it. This is a thin Tuesday night
in the town of your birth, in October,
a breech and bruising birth, for which
your mother has never quite forgiven you.

You are looking for old friends in a strange pub.
If you asked, the barman would point people out.
The one with his foot in his mouth, laughing.
The one with the face like a wet Wakes Week.
You sit in the corner alone. The songs pass
like years. You search for something good

to put on, but there's not even Elvis.
In this pub at least Elvis is still and always
dead, a small excuse for their dad's sideburns.
The Massed Beer Mat Flippers of Bamber Bridge
are all the welcome home you can find,
and nobody, but nobody recognizes you.

You start to draw the road out of here,
but it will dry on the table and leave a slug trail
that will give you away. Your parents will find you.
The Flippers grin as if in on one of your secrets,
that even you have forgotten: the silhouettes
inside a tent at a party, the wild gossip in the house.

As you leave you see the buses cross the bridge
into town, splashing the puddles into the river.
The water drops through the bridge's dark shadow
like rain onto the taut canvas of that tent,
the slap like the feet of a man running, running,
a series of nails driven rapidly home.

Between the cat food and the secateurs

my reflection winks back from a cracked wing mirror,
out in the garage, beating a hollow into a pile of papers.
The dark outside disapproves of the figure I cut
while you are coping, the rhythm that I've set up.

Fuck it. If I knew what to say next,
when I stick my head on a pole and offer it
through the back door as an apology, I wouldn't be here.
I wouldn't have bothered to have muddied my shoes.

Wind blows through the rowing machine that couldn't
get rid of my beer gut. The hammering from a
                neighbour's shed
echoes my thrashing the headlines, drops into the hole
I'm ripping into this four-foot pile of bad news,
                ridiculous.

The Neighbourhood Watch peeps through the cat flap,
                concerned.
Go home, please. There's nothing to see now.
A drunken man contemplating the differences
between a monkey wrench and a tin opener.

Something vague has something me

I'm not sure when and don't care to check.
Sometime between that first kiss in the damp
and swirling basement of Everton Boys Club
and now, this soggy mass of in-between
that feels all the time like afterwards.

Let this spoil our late-night reading of the papers:
you are what you do, not what you dream of doing.
Our dreams most would not recognize if
they waved a flag, which they do: a big red one
with a picture of James Brown and Elvis on it.

Glasses half-empty, or full, whatever, we're drunk
and bent on uncovering the truth to all this.
This is my dream: us together naked
in a railway-station photo booth after midnight,
and while we wait for the photos to slide out,

phallic and glistening, ready to steal our fingerprints,
delayed passengers queue to pat us on the back
and scribble on our goose-bumped flesh
with indelible marker pens. 'Dreamers' it says
on my thighs and across your shoulders.

Meanwhile, outside in our dreams and outside
in our drunkenness, the day whips its energies
into a whirlwind with us at its centre.
We're not the centre of anything, we blush,
but it takes not a blind bit of notice.

Song III

Give him a hammer to seal his window.
Give him a bag to hide his head.
Give him a sock to seal his mouth.
Give him an axe for under the bed.
If the bastard's not guilty, why is he bleeding?

Take his TV and beat it to bits.
Take his diaries and show them around.
Take his good name and use it in vain.
Take his secrets and make sure they're found.
If the bastard's not guilty, why is he bleeding?

Make his money earn its keep.
Make his smile seem winning.
Make his story almost dull.
Make his lies like sinning.
If the bastard's not guilty, why is he bleeding?

And if he squeals don't let him go.
And if he ask don't let him know.
And if he weeps don't let tears flow.
And if he denies show him it's so.
If the bastard's not guilty, why is he bleeding?

After eighteen years of this sort of thing

I will put my best heart forward and hope
for a dip in the attentions of the day.
The rational city plays a peeping game
behind the headlines and the U-turns,
our friends' necessary betrayals.

The reversals, the blockage, the lost
and irreplaceable gather at our gate,
like snails that crunch under the children's feet.
The afternoon feels like an in-joke
no one can fully explain. I'm so tired

of being English in this shabby excuse
for what might be, so thoroughly tired
of feeling like a man questioning the rules
of cricket or football – why *can't* he touch it
with his hand? – I can hardly breathe these words.

But if I've inherited one thing from
my family it's a stubborn streak as wide
as the Ribble. I am going to sit here until
the image of Portillo at the stake
disappears from my morbid mind.

And then tomorrow you and I will take the kids
to the allotment, where we will plant sunflowers
on our communal land to mark the beginning
of the end. To such small victories am I reduced.
The light fades suddenly, is swallowed by evening.

I think of you with nothing on,

the shyness and boldness of curves
that have tipped me up and swung me round
until my head was full of ringing feedback
and those arched and tempting eyebrows
luring us over a faintly marked border
into the autumn-soaked field of the new.

I think of you and miss you now, the pot
of your belly that fits into my hot palm,
the unregarded navel wrinkled and winking,
self-conscious from two dramatic labours,
like a pruning scar on the bole of a tree,
the symmetry of stretch marks on hips

and belly, silver stabs of tensions that pull
and grow even now when the children tug away,
that concertina to next to nothing, a rouche
of darker skin that curls back from my fingertips,
a tenderness we dare hardly speak,
until you lie down and all lines shift.

I have started to thicken, to set
into the shape of my dad, can feel
the temptation grow to whip out my denture
at a quiet unexpected moment, the way
my granddad used to, to embarrass my nan.
I'm holding my belly in as I write this

so you won't misunderstand: I think of you
and want you here to pose this question:
haven't these concessions been worth it?
It's hard to believe this nakedness,
or the thought of it, won't lead somewhere,
isn't an image for how we must carry on.

I've half a mind, and that's all I need,

to turn this street upside down
and hide in the warmth of ignorance,
not a thought for how the light squeezed
from good homes drains down, disappears
through the sloping grass to the river.

I could sit here and ghost a stranger's life,
slip in some things I've admitted to no one,
cross my fingers certain people never read it.
You. Moving through events not your own
you can slip off the shackles a while.

I can ramble on until I meet this stranger's
friends, his lovers. In a place that feels
like a corner I find his family huddled together
for warmth, though they are bickering fiercely.
They're making up insulting names for him, or me.

I'm so tired you could snuff me out
with a simple bringing together of your thumb
and forefinger. It wouldn't even hurt.
This street is no duller than any other
in England, but it rankles. The sun

ducking down beyond the park is like
a smear of egg yoke on a child's bib.
The dusk goes into meltdown, into
feedback, and then it starts to rain,
big, petulant globs of rain that in a minute

turn to hail and back again, to tattoo
a state-of-the-nation broadcast
down the back of my neck, that's steam
in a moment and heard no more.
I've half a mind, and that's all I need...

The sea's rising arc

wipes its mouth on our sentimental gaze,
chucks its spume and spleen our way
till we are forced back to the car.
The children bicker over the head of some toy.

We ignore them. It's cold and getting colder.
On the shore the waves are building to a riot
of pointless fury, mob after justified mob
wanting payback for some ancient grievance.

There are lost souls flying above the sand,
crimped and chapped from desperate scrubbing.
We can even hear them breathing in the car
when the children fall asleep, in the background

to our silence, breath so shallow it's like that
of the man pulled dead from a freezing sea,
just waiting to thaw, only they buried him,
heard him jerk awake, skin his brow on the coffin lid.

We're about to admit something we shouldn't,
but the wind catches it and throws it into the sea.
It's hard to know how you felt so long ago,
but if you can, we do. We start to laugh at ourselves:

the white frenzy the sea knocks itself into
seems almost blue as the windows steam up
and we can't do what we dream of doing,
even if the kids are asleep. We just can't.

I'll accept the testimony of the river,

its improbable stories about the future
that last forever, the fields now under
the floodwaters. A cloud smothers the moon:
like a security light clicking off.
The river slips its arm around the park

in a drunken gesture of comradeship.
You're always telling me things will work out.
The cold air's slap has stopped me laughing.
The dew starts to bend the grass back, I could
write an epic poem with my foot or wait

to carve it from the dirt on the car boot.
Looking back toward the house I see
the Pelican Crossing run through its
simple sequence like a nervous actor
learning his one line late into the night.

Uncertainties, mysteries, doubts
cluster in what remains of the light,
like the patterns of dust revealed
when a man you were polling leant against his door
and let the brightness of his home interrogate you.

The road is jealous of the river's chat.
At the back of my throat a tiny shadow
mimics these words, fingers twisting, sliding,
cracking though they have no bones.
'All the better to mock you with.'

The family as the first soviet and other daft ideas

swim through my lustful yearnings, my jealousy
of the frustrated certainties of the old comrades.
It all saps the imagination: I can't embroider this
into something complicated, but there's an idea I have
that beneath the surface of the town I shop in

there's another that looks the same but feels
different. Where all the stubbornness and bile
hardens into ornately carved bricks describing
the odd shrinking feeling that buried itself deep,
deep within your chest during the adverts.

In the park this morning we sped down the hill
on some old For Sale signs and a huge bin bag,
bounced over compacted snow picking up speed,
yelling and holding on to each other as we hit the fence
at the bottom erected to protect the fish farm.

Though we battered it with our accelerating feet
and our cries, it tilted but did not fall.
I wanted us to slide on and out over the water,
you with our son, and me with our daughter,
over the frozen river, our gloves rubbed smooth

as we skimmed the ice and headed out
to startle the sheep, anywhere out of here,
with the rest of the country following.
This may be vague, impractical and sentimental,
but it does not feel it.

If I waste time thinking

of how the songs of the clouds
are writing their cheerful selves down river,
full of anger and historic bottom,
striving to make shapes they never quite manage,
how am I going to get down to breakfast?

There's a dog in the middle of the lawn
barking and barking, chipping away
at the nostalgic picture the houses
on the ragged horizon so desperately sketch.
Too small to be threatening, it skirts the garden
translating the sarcastic messages of our cats.

Each morning, gravity has added another line
to your beautiful face. Each has this to say,
in its different and delightful way:
'This woman is knackered but smiles a lot.'
The kids are minor miracles, or earthquakes,
throbbing with inspiration I can only guess at.

'We have run out of granola, it will have to be
toast or nothing,' you shout. The coffee is as bitter
as the news is bland. 'That's how I like to start the day,'
I say, almost joking. If I wasn't aggressive
I don't know what I would be. I'm sorry.
Somewhere in the kitchen a definition of grace is hiding.

We would have a better chance of finding it
if one of our mothers lived round the corner.
By such flat and cardboard details are
the dimensions of our spiritual life confined.
You'd laugh to see me typing the words
spiritual life. I'm laughing now.

Please come in and disturb me.

Like an illustration in a children's book

the washing drips in the disparate dusk,
an endless hiatus on the paving stones, dot
after hanging dot widening to circles of damp.
The church bell nags stubbornly at the hour,
keen for souls to save. Ours are doomed
to crease like shirts I hang too hurriedly.

We've been searching for something dull,
like an alarm clock, but not that. If we could remember
what it was, we'd at least know where to start.
An hour spent turning the bathroom upside down,
then we're drawn at scrubbing at smudges
of toothpaste eating away at our new varnish.

The smell of nappies has returned from nowhere,
just wont be scratched from beneath our nails.
Creating a new landscape on the patio,
from mud and compost and heaps of daffodils,
in tantrum-filled abstract expressions of joy
the children out-do us at everything.

They skid and run from apple tree to garage
and scream. Not without aggression they push us
against the garage wall so we cannot work.
I have felt forgiveness shrink in me
like an unused organ and been terrified.
I have hidden my anger in folds of wind

but now I am ready to pack away this disillusion.
Look at the last of the sun on the children's legs,
the way it has nothing at all to do with these things
more complex than heat, light, smoothness
of skin that has hardly begun to age. Another
enthusiastic misunderstanding I may live to regret.

Walking the gaps between hills

the children are gripped by a sudden calm.
Hand in hand they profess in approximate words
their love for each other, turned by some trick
of this polluted light into giants
striding on our behalf out of this world,
anywhere innocence is not ironic.

The humps of green are melting into autumn,
the odd bare line shyly scratches itself
on our memories of this long hot summer.
In the valley the sky's a day away
and the sea just a persistent rumour.
The horses in the fields aren't at all puzzled.

As the slope steepens we can see the kids'
legs start to bend with the effort, as if
the statues we would make of them were top heavy,
had legs of papiermaché and torses of stone.
We scoop them up and driven impulsive by hope
race them screaming to the top of the hill.

Nature, someone else's Great Lost Cause,
tries to underline the lesson of all this,
but I'm too stupid to see it. I can feel
my life gathering pace like a stone dislodged
by our running, tumbling down the hill,
desperate for a use to put its falling weight to.

Rolled on the floor and still laughing we look down
on the towns below us, the coils and knots of pipes
and chimneys, the clouds of smoke that seamlessly
knit into the sea-fret, terraces like dominoes
waiting to fall in spectacular sequence, the finale
to a festival we are all invited to.

One fitful night after a trying evening

you dream there's this one life and all you have to do
is open the door to find it there on the step,
fresh and fashionable as a milk bottle full of orange
            juice.
The unanswerable hunger you wake with is deadly,

the day's an idea dismissed as unreasonable
and there's nothing surprising about the news any more.
The bedspread lies in argumentative knots
over clothes performing poor impressions of our
            charms.

It matters we remember what we were feeling
when careless we threw them to the floor but we can't.
It matters how we touched then on something
we'd forgotten. It seems to matter that the day

begins like this, opens like the bitter flower
in the white jug on our wooden table, beneath
the window that soaks up the sun like a sponge
licks away spilt white wine and the words that spilt it.

The one life you dream of starts with a squall of children,
of moods and merriment. It's an odd shape, for sure,
but as the day gathers pace and runs away from us,
            again,
and the summer breaks its fall on the garden,

this naïve daub of a life has a power of its own and
the square of sky the window shows is all that we
            expected,
blue as our eyes, and our children's eyes, endless
as the heat that draws and binds this moment together.

Song VI

Glad up to my elbows
Gladder down to my knees
My chest is a fresh-baked loaf of bread
My brow is crammed with tunes
Is that a hyperbole in your pocket
Or are you just pleased to see me?

Glad up to my tonsils
Gladder down to my segs
My skin is a suit called Tingle
My smile is a twist of lime
Is that a metaphor in your pocket
Or are you just pleased to see me?

Glad up to my earlobes
Gladder down to my calves
My spleen is a stone to sit upon
My heart is a sea-whipped shell
Is that a paradox in your pocket
Or are you just pleased to see me?

Glad up to my screaming
Gladder down to my moans
My eyes suck juice from oranges
My hands sculpt great promises
Is that a smirk in your pocket
Or are you just pleased to see me?

Bringing Down The Government
(Epilogue – 1997)

The wicker chair we'd seen by the skip was gone.
I sat in the space we'd cleared for it and watched
as you topped and tailed the peas, nipping the ends
with the scars you call your fingernails. We cursed
our luck, our place in things, the sods that beat us
to this rare chance to better ourselves. We laughed.

The lifestyle issue, raised again, got laughed
out of the crumbling house, but now it's gone
we want it back – somehow it means a lot to us.
Knowing how much we watch our lives, how watched
they sour like gooseberry wine that's cursed
to turn to vinegar before the summer ends,

when the peas are done we walk to the ends
of our lands, some twenty-five yards of laughed-
and lived-in ground. The children have cursed
the garage with scribble that will soon be gone.
Our daughter waves from the tree, she watched,
she tries to say, while we thought only of us,

the day before yesterday when there was only us.
So this reverie and its quiet talk ends
and we return to the case at hand, watched
by her eager eyes that flashed and laughed
their way through the morning that's now gone.
When we look back, maybe these days will seem curse

by over-ambition. Still, the only curse
apparent's the one that rips time from us.
The restraint that plagued us suddenly gone
we realize we didn't notice it end.
Did it simply dissolve while we laughed
at it, or did it slip away as we watched

for each other's tensions and oddities, watched
for the signs of silently becoming cursed
to live out ordinary days, the ones we laughed
our way out of when younger? 'It was us
that decided to live like this,' our silence ends
by saying, before the children ensure it's gone.

And if anybody watched the two of us
would we be cursed for the simple ends
we turn our laughed-in lives to? When we're gone?

from Gaps Between Hills (1996)

From the shadow of the flats

beyond the bridge of the hills the flash of white water
        the arbor of steel the ridges of bark
beyond the nipples of chimneys the rake of the chute
        the slush of the neon the chink of the till
beyond the tattoo of hunger the breath of a dream

beyond the forest of plumes the chase of the beach
        the gang of rough gardens the shelter of scrub land
beyond the gamble of hedges the fist of hydrangeas
        the stain of wire fences the field of lost toddlers
beyond the slag of graffiti the breath of a dream

beyond the tic of late giros the whine of the pavements
        the smelting of scratch cards the gag of nappies
beyond the slave-song of mowers the coda of bad chests
        the pit of the weekend the cracking of locks
beyond the wheeze of sunday the breath of a dream

beyond the arc of a football the breath of a dream
beyond the clean sweep of river the breath of a dream
beyond the spray of red sun the breath of a dream
beyond the white noise of surf the breath of a dream
beyond the reach of our shadows the breath of a dream

lungs catching new air breath of a dream

Rio de Juninho

We could have had a gritty midfield battler,
cast from the bits British Steel had left over,
last welding done by a returner from Saudi,
dragged from Grangetown by a traveller's pony,
his forehead trailing on the dirty tarmac,
a matter of inches from his hairy knuckles,
his mam and dad proud and loud in the stand
when his prehensile studs rip thoroughly through
the arty-farty shins of a Dutch dazzler,

or a rough and tumble striker on the way up,
thick as a brick made of slag but big hearted,
with a forehead like a stoker's shovel
and sharpened elbows that have been known
to carve his names in defenders' backsides,
whose first words as a child were translated as
'I'll bite your bloody balls off you big arsewipe,'
with his right foot as true as his tax returns,

but then we would not have seen,
walking by the still filthy river one day,
ten thousand yellow shirts dancing in the breeze,
a new look in people's eyes,
something not to be denied even by results,
that I know is ridiculous but still want,
a dreaming set off like a ticking bomb,
this chipped and battered town
twinned with a place so exotic
we did not know it was just like home.

We like it here: Song of a Lazenby Bull

Working out why the grass turns brown
as the earth mumbles beneath you
can sap the *joie de vivre* from even
the toughest hide, the most ruminant soul.
I savour every blade of grass as a bonus, twice.

But we like it here, low like the works' alarms
when warm rain crackles down our leather.
Steaming nostrils taste the wind, feel it
blow its crazed and cobbled answers past,
and elaborate string of coded excuses.

When the opaque sky allows a gobbet of sun
I close my eyes and feel like dancing,
posing for a snapshot to use on a postcard,
that must always say 'Glad you're not here,
having a brilliant time without you.'

The tingle in my brow grows, horns of smoke
plume out above my head, everything starts
to make a little sense, as my shadow wobbles
over the scrub towards the works
to demand an explanation for this confusing joy.

As we continue our search for pomegranates

the rain drenches the crowded market stalls
with all the descriptive detail it can muster.
Sometimes home can be the most exotic place
there is, the shoppers faces as wrinkled
and misshapen, as fascinating as the oldest
babushkas in the remotest Uzbeki village.

Today is not one of those days. Today
is a shop for fruit and get the hell out day.
Buskers stare forlornly from Barrat's
doorway, weighing up the pros and cons
of electrocution, their chances of survival.
The pineapples, girls, are guaranteed sweet.

The pomegranates in their boxes nestle
in shredded raffia, hold more promises
than anyone could ever keep. They'll spill
their bitty regrets into the folds of your shirt,
will stain it the colour of my bitten lips.
In the morning you'll wonder how that happened.

The *Gazette* shouts, or at least raises its voices,
to tell us of cheap gas, plummeting power prices.
There is no power here, no power at all.
Today is one of those days the town seems
inhabited purely by stroke victims, ourselves
included. We poke each other in the ribs:

it's like being seventeen again, drifting
round cafés bored and superior. We're not.
There's something difficult and puzzling
about the sequence of the traffic lights
at the crossroads: we find ourselves stranded,
hold out our hands as if to check it's still raining.

Pair of little pig poems for Dermot Blackburn

1. Pig Shelters, Eston Hills

The wind frisks the hillside for warmth.
Stepping stones beneath a ribcage of cloud,
knuckle bone dice deciding stay or go,
this hamlet stays where hunger put it.

All the little piggies have gone wearily home.
An abandoned shelter shows its belly
to the blue, a coracle miles from water.
The snow's rough lace grows tight with frost.

2. Leaving his tin shed like a beetle on its back,

this little piggy took the hugeness of the sky
for a sign that he should say goodbye,

took the snow for a blank page in a jotter,
scratched a farewell note with nervous trotter:

'Thanks for having me. I enjoyed the views.
You know where I'll be if you have any news.'

Low

The must of cow parsley froths
at paths our tread keeps down
to gravel,

that tomorrow will be littered
with the shed skins that hope
let fall,

blown there by a low wind
searching for a dim corner
to hide in.

from The Horse Burning Park (1994)

The Horse Burning Park

It's fun for all the family.
Real horses, real fat to fly
past your pink little ears.
Real aroma to tickle the hairs
of your ever so delicate noses.
Real flames to singe your trousers.

The incredible heritage of horse burning.

We'll take you through the theory and the practice.
We'll stroll through a living, breathing, burning museum:
horse burning through the ages.
Some of you might find the methods used barbaric.
Here at The Park, we think them quaint.
Simplicity in everything,
especially horse burning.
That was the motto of my forefathers.
My family have been burning horses for six generations.
The lengths I have to go to burn a horse nowadays.
My grandfather would have died laughing.
And they do say I'm to be the last allowed to burn horses.
What my son will do I don't know.
Taking tours around a museum is no way to live.

But I digress.
Shall we start.

That one belonged to Boedicia.
It gazed upon her breasts, so was burnt.
Gazed, not grazed, madam.
The method is classically simple.
They simply shove the horse onto
the nearest bonfire and poke it
so that it stays in the flames.
Once the legs have gone,
you're laughing.

They're doing a good job, those men,
do try and appreciate it.
Craftsmen the like of which we don't get today.

Yes, this particular method stems from a time
when horses were burnt to warm the house.
A little too utilitarian for my liking.
No art in it, just heating.
Of course, fireplaces were bigger then.
The children used to pick through the ashes
looking for teeth and play a game
rather similar to marbles with them.

Any questions so far?

There may be a little pain involved,
but not as we understand it.
Horses are beautiful animals, but unintelligent.

Yes, posters and t-shirts are available,
along with technical histories of the art
and novels and autobiographies of some
of its 'characters', such as Nathan Churles,
who personally rode every horse before burning it,
and thatched his cottage with their manes,
forcing his wife, Nellie, to comb it daily.

No, the horses were in actual fact
burnt indoors, in 'burning sheds'.
The Park is an attempt to capture
the excitement without the grime.

Yes, I would rather be burning horses
than standing here talking to you.

Trafalgar Square 1990

The problem starts when you're
in front of the mirror trying on
the prophetic voice for size.
There's an awkward silence
while you search for the next line,
filled only by the sun filtering
through the blinds like in an ad.
The damned thing just won't be writ.

The news provides the punch-line
but kills the rest, proving grounded
fears you bored yourself with.
Smashed windows and cameramen
rapidly revise Eastern Europe's
sympathetic camera angles,
under orders to get a more British
view of the proceedings.

The next line never does come,
and you're left wondering
about eggs and omelettes,
Keat's "like a leaf to a tree",
while the sun filters through
like news at once good and bad,
and the street cleaners move in
grumbling and totting up overtime.

Nowhere to Hide

It is not the simple presence of evil that is unbearable;
what is unbearable is the impossibility of reconciling the
facts of evil with the beauty of the world.
Greil Marcus on Robert Johnson

There's a line of hate running down my spine
and into the street, threading through this town
like a tapeworm. There's but one thin wall between me
and an alien place where black bags sprout
on Monday nights, carelessly tied, spilling crap,
where the Jags stop dead in the middle of the road,
engines smoking, to pick up the piecework from
housebound wives who jingle the change they've earned
in callused hands smaller than their husbands',
stronger than the kids', so far.

Tabloid daydreams and a fitting lack of imagination
match like a bad carpet and a worse settee.
Those others with the supplement lifestyles,
they're a good few streets away, and I hate them too,
Take up thy spleen and heal thyself, some dupe says,
trying to take the piss and failing, just asking
for a smack in the teeth. But I got distracted
by the wind as it changed and caught the familiar smell
of the Asian house on the corner burning.

L-O-V-E   H-A-T-E
flash before my eyes, constants, as I flip over
Greatest Hits, crank up the volume, and make
The Vandellas transmute love into hate and back again.
The transport of those voices, does that make pain
noble? I am dancing but my hands are scarred forever.
The line of hate runs through a muddle of hope.
The music drowns out the news, but not the facts
about misery, loss and the youth of today's
strange taste in trousers, pin-ups and so-called ethics.

Bile duct on permanent overdrive? Well, who would
deny me that? I make myself feel more worthy
by saving cardboard boxes for the bright-eyed girls
who sleep and wake beneath the railway bridges,
where survivors turn debris into futures.
I've a line of hate from my pulsing temple
to that of the wife-beater across the way,
and his wife for letting him live. I'd move
but there's *nowhere to run to* –

People round here are very accepting.

A pointless display of unmarketable skills

The echo of my footsteps down the street
is not the echo of my footsteps down the street
but the slippery flip flop slap of a drunk.

Chimneys pull the moon around, turn it on
and off as I walk down to an unsold house.
A car pulls away from the Spar in a crunch

of glass and wood. The corner's littered
with laughter, and a squall of brakes sets
me up for a series of falters and falls.

The lads did their homework, picked a shop
topped with dead-end deadpan blank-faced flats
to entice photographers to their nearest thing

to a good time, to that belter of a bad joke
they somehow wring from a school-stunted vocabulary
and a Peer School Ph.D. in car chases.

Wondering at the fun on the far side
of a vicious streak of nothing, I snigger
at the vulgarity of news come home to roost;

I plod back beside that unthreatening drunk
as sirens raise voices in an edgy neighbourhood
soon to become fashionable.

Voice from the settee

Those yellowed sheets of old news in drawers
in the dustiest room of my Nan's house,
how did they get that way? I start to understand.

I hear the theme tune to *Match of the Day*
slipping up the stairs to entice me down
again to get done, get sent back to fume,
and all because of my much younger sister –
I can feel it fit in. Through the debris of years
that clog the child I was I am edging towards
a solution, though it may not be pretty. Tell me
something about the way my parents seemed
to walk slower and slower until they just stopped,
more or less, and I'll thank you.
Give me something even approaching a reason
and I'll give you more, in the same spirit
my dad gave those years to the warehouse.
The clothes and chairs of the aging workers leave
me moved, wondering how I got out, what happened.

Those drawers of my Nan's, those slips she must
have been young and frivolous in, once; the smell
of that dusty-aired spare room my sister and I
shared while my parents were out on the town;
the walk down the road leading past the gasworks,
over the playing fields of the school that lined me up
for parsing, rugby and refinement of the soul
throughout my teens, past the spot still scorched
by the pickets' brazier, the blood long since
washed away with the jobs, the walk that ends
in the corner of the field where Mickey Thorne lost
his virginity to the girl with a baby by the 3rd year,
the walk past the vicarage whose windows we smashed;
Mee's Children's Encyclopedia that turned up years later
in a subsequent house with no memories attached,
the margins full of scribbled nonsense, daydreams,
if you can get me all of these things in the same picture,

I'll be grateful, I'll be renewed, and you can have
my copy of *Match of the Day: Great Goals of the 1970s*.
It's never out of the video these long winter afternoons
of nothing to do and no sun, and no other options.
Only now do I start to see why, as the tape rewinds
to Charlie George on his back waiting to be kissed.
The world is a place that has changed and I need
        your help.

J'ai rêvé tellement fort de toi

after Robert Desnos in Terezin

Our dreams were so full of each other
that the love we spoke of so often
has outgrown our clumsy human hands,
become strange to us, a thing un-known.

I, who loved even your shadow too much,
am left little but a charcoal-drawn likeness
to hold against the pressing dark.
The sustaining myth of eternal love.

When you are dressing in the half-dawn
in the damp of early summer, it's me,
the shadow lurking behind the wardrobe door
as it swings and creaks to clothe you,

it's me.

Becoming short-sighted

The more I look out at the world
the harder it gets to see across the street.

The houses opposite fog over, that new couple
moving down a rickety ladder are lost to a blur

that dances around focus but decides on nothing.
We'll not get to know them. I'd put money on it.

This lunchtime's obsession is the fresh plans for schools:
Get rich quick or stay thick, the white paper's called.

(They've stopped even pretending.) If there are angry
              crowds
gathering in the gloom only yards away I can't see them.

One explanation

The ghosts of the street are angry
that Jeanne's closed down the shop.
You can feel them through holes in the wind
weaving curses on Sainsbury's.

She's gone back to being a nurse.
We never have crumpets for tea now,
have to pay £2.69 for Bulgarian red,
run out of matches with no pilot light.

The ghosts of the street confer
with animals and children
to get something done.
That's the tension you can feel.

Boom slump boom slump...

Life not like it was in the adverts:
just the lingering smell of sherry,
the prospect of tumbling motionless
into a coma on the cat-scratched sofa
after another fruitless twelve-hour day.

I am standing at the window wondering
what I was thinking two minutes ago.

It was important, I know it was, it was
a good idea of some sort, something to undo
a few knots in our ragged shoelaces,
tick off a few boxes on our list of things
to do to make life bearable – but it's gone.

It vanished just like that, behind the moon
I was enjoying so much, and before you know
it'll be next week, and I'll still not have said
anything about how good your meals are,
or the million ways you can smile when
you let yourself. I'll have slept all weekend.

I move without knowing it, talk without
thinking or feeling, and you don't notice
when I ask you to rub the parts of me
that have gone dead. I twitch with tiredness,
feet moving the cushions, unearthing some
of what brought us here. The moon is nowhere,
as unheard as the trains that speed through Europe
in a strop, economic refugees leaping in and out
of all available windows, to bring a leveling down
I am convinced is a moral imperative but then
my hours get accordingly longer, less lucrative,
and life together shrinks to sleep and some desperate
pleasures: arguing mostly, and counting blessings.

When the wind changed direction six months ago
we were in a good patch, we see now.
We both neared home with a smile, thinking
of things we couldn't even picture once.
This was happening elsewhere, to someone else.
Did it feel right though? Of course it did.

It will happen again, don't worry.
Somewhere there's a speculator tearing
petals from a rose wilting on his desk:
She loves him She loves him not
She loves him She loves him not
She loves him

Struggling

I haven't had time to stand and fart recently,
and you're wanting me to work on a relationship?

That silence gathering in the front room
like a crowd waiting for a drunk to fall,

it's something to do with you, isn't it?
Some kind of comment, some kind of rebuke?

Poverty appears like steam, after growing
invisibly, takes its shapes when it meets the cold.

I've been spinning on the spot like a mad dog
trying to make two short ends meet, and I don't

need advice on how to feel happier
on less, thank you very much. Passing

on the street, no-one would know, except
that I am hurrying, from one tired place

to another, wearing out cheap shoes faster
than the rest of town. I'm struggling.

Portrait of the artist as an embarrassment

Riffling the pages on someone else's
favourite book, you found a faded note
telling you what to do with your life.

'I can't believe in flowery words,
couldn't say or see anything *like*
anything else anymore. I'm ready

to call it a problem if you do.
The placing of blame I never even
considered till you mentioned it.

Vagueness, its attractions and dangers,
discuss.' You were younger then, granted,
but the plan drawn-up has stayed only that.

The future you remember is hidden
somewhere at the back of a cupboard
in a house you left quickly years ago –

a hope fallen slowly away

as you grow clearer-headed, less likely to return
and find it now makes you blush, like a bad photo
that caught you unawares, with a silly haircut.

Poem from a distance

The mud in the air in this town
gets under your skin, and John
is growing obsessed with that photo
of Dylan where he has John's new haircut.

They pass too many bottles around the park
before they all move on to where no-one
but Mark has ever been known to cop off.
When they're not dancing, they're at the bar.

'We *are* going to have to get out,
you do realise that, don't you?'
someone asks as they zig-zag home.
'You look nothing like Dylan, at any age.

I'm afraid for us all.' Cue laughter,
choking, falling into the road, etcetera.

Buttocks

The darkness leads us away from our goals.
Fearing the stone beneath our knees
we crawl one after another, grimly holding
onto the buttocks of an incomplete stranger,
forming a line through the darkness,
a line of buttock-holding strangers.
There is absolutely no fondling for fun.
We inch our way forward, slowly,
straying from our path several times.
Occasionally an anguished cry is heard.
Someone has lost hold of a buttock.
None of us know just whose buttocks we are holding,
if they are kind, friendly, lonely, happy or sad.
Somewhere up ahead is the light at the end of the tunnel.
Exactly which tunnel we have all forgotten.
We have also forgotten why we are in which ever tunnel this is.
There is no room for memory or contemplation.
Immense concentration is required to keep hold
of an unknown buttock for a lifetime.

Breaking House Rule No 1

for Alison

That we'd drawn a line, thick as our heads
would be tomorrow morning, didn't mean, you said,

that we weren't about to cross it. And then
that great soca tune, *Hot Hot Hot*, said 'when',

moments after the glass had overflowed.
As we surfaced, Big Sue from down the road

asked for the lights to go on – she had lost
her false teeth. Our hiding eyes were embossed

with that central bulb, the floundering dancers,
and our housemates fixing questions to answers.

The taxi home was awkwardly silent.
Peter said something to Deb: we knew what he meant.

Nothing else happened that night – who knows how?
We laugh and wonder at our restraint even now.

Tying the knot

take the two ends –
grip them hard
as if you mean it –
bring them together
then cross them
put one end through the loop
you have made, then pull

at this stage you must say
'I never thought - '

pull the two ends
in opposite directions
as hard as you possibly can
the strain should show
repeat the process
until face muscles twitch
and your arms ache

take care to say
'I never meant - '

it might sound hard work
but it is worth it
remember to be tender
the result may not be pretty
but it will be effective
knots aren't made to be pretty
they are meant to be tight

when you have finished
say sorry

The Domesticity Remix

'Well, yes, we do own our own house,
but we don't dust it very often.'

By the time Chuck D shuts it, and tells Terminator X
to let rip, the washing up's done and dried.

Somehow the smell of fried onions the perfect side
of almost burnt gets across something of contented excess,

through the noise of the beat breaking, through the shape
of arguments we'll now never have. *'Suckers to the side*

I know you hate – my 98 – (You're gonna get yours!)' Bite
our lips as we do, about different difficult pasts, late

night dancing round the living room proves one thing:
we didn't know we were born in that time whose borders
          are sealed,

tight as catering plasters and as bruise blue, healed
cuts thankful for the dark that forgetting or silence bring.

'Brothers and sisters, I don't know what this world is coming to.'
We feel like eight cans of 44p Spar bitter in an hour,

but tonight in our tiredness by a reluctant fire
neither will leave the house, neither can see how days grew

so dim so quickly. To a beat to crush eggshells, absurd, we
          avoid
the footsteps of our parents. Without us even noticing

our baby has crawled to the stairs, and is stretching and
          climbing.
We are punching the air with Flavor Flav, too happy to be
          alarmed.

God Save The Queen

'There is no future in England's dreaming'
Sex Pistols

'Il y a en nous un si profond silence'
Phillippe Jaccottet

There is in us a silence so deep
a stone falling would not dent it.
This stark music, broad and strong
as the world hard and cruel, only hides
in noise our knowledge that bad things
happen unremarked if this is as good
as it gets. It's something, but it's not
enough, treasured vinyl in tattered sleeves.

Are we alive? To prove it we swear
through a clatter of guitars, spittingly happy,
full into the face of the future, whatever.
That same song heard in a club years ago,
shocked in a a sweating frenzy of friends,
hints again at the uselessness of art:
how the hell did I end up here, regressing
to escape plans and tantrums in the chaos surging
round the chorus like a bitter but useful row.
As the needle clicks to a halt there is a silence
for us to sway in, then the rest of our lives.

There is no one for us to blame
if the stone hits our hidden room.

Making curry with Marvin Gaye & Tammi Terrell

The rash sun and patient moon are no more like our two hearts
than budgies in a cage squabbling over some old cuttlefish.

After 30 seconds in hot oil, the mustard seeds have sizzled
with as much life as they had, have paled into still pungent grey.
The chilli fades like a lawn in a long dry summer, storing fire.

You have got both troublesome children to sleep at the same
    time.
This is an achievement to match my Bengan Bhaji. I keep
    rewinding
our ancient tape to the first verse of *Ain't No Mountain High
    Enough*
where Tammi leans into the song, dipping her doomed
    shoulder,
*If you need me call me, no matter where you are, no matter
    how far.*

I keep confusing the thrill of great pop music with being in love.
That drives you mad, I know. I'm not apologising.

The wise and beautiful moon at the bottom of our garden makes
    us shiver,
like this lager, like we did in the fog, in the back of your Mum's
    Metro,
a mid-Pennine lay-by, in the days before the children taught us
    what tired meant.
It's the way the cashews speckle the basmati, soft as my tongue on
    yours,
and the aubergines, most of all it's the aubergines, that prove to
    you
what Marvin and Tammi have just shown me, yet again:
the days may feel as if they last an hour too long,
but they are finely tuned to hold just enough happiness
to send us ready and willing into the next.

The heat spreading from my fingertips demands the last word:
the perfect length for most things is three minutes
and one fine day we'll cut our time together down to that.
Let's practice by listening to this song one more time before
            we eat.

Domestic Bliss

The mess gets worse as the beautiful world
tries harder, expands on its original mistake –
something crass blurted out in a fluster –
making a mountain out of moleshit.

You and I aren't bothered. Too busy to
beat the wolves from the doorstep, too tired
to be pissed off about anything, tonight
the blackcurrant wine is dying our tongues

the colour of our hearts. We're saying what we mean,
for once, and it feels good, making plans
for the future as if there were no tomorrow.
Your smile leaps out from behind your teeth.

We can do whatever we want.
What we want to do now is
get sordid in front of the fire.
The world is hard but worth it.

Acknowledgements

Some of these poems were first published in the following collections: *The Horse Burning Park* (Stride), *Half A Mind* (Flambard), *Gaps Between Hills* (Scratch) and *A Balkan Exchange* (Arc). Many thanks to Rupert Loydell, Margaret and Peter Lewis and Tony Ward. Thanks also to Kevin Cadwallender for publishing my first pamphlet in 1990. Thanks to Andy Croft, Dermot Blackburn, Bill Herbert, Linda France, Nadia Radulova, VBV, Georgi Gospodinov and Kristin Dimitrova for collaborating on the latter two books, especially Dermot for the photographs.

Thanks are due to the editors of the following magazines and anthologies where some of the previously uncollected poems first appeared: *Leviathan Quarterly, The North, Prop, The Rialto, Samizdat, Slope, Stride Magazine, Hasty, Magnetic North* (New Writing North), *North by North East* (Iron Press), *Smelter* (Mudfog Press), *Voices for Kosovo* (Stride).

'By rote' was adapted for use in *Remember the Future*, a short film for Tyne Tees Television, produced by A19 Films; thanks to Belinda Williams and Nick Oldham. 'A new guide to Seaton Carew' was commissioned by Cleveland Arts and published in *Seaton Carew Daytrips*; thanks to Bob Beagrie. 'Basho Visits the Headland, Hartlepool' was discovered in the *Book of the North*, an exhibition and cd-rom project put together by Bill Herbert and Claire Malcolm at New Writing North, back when cd-roms were cutting edge; thanks to them both, and to the other artists and writers involved. 'Imagine a city' was written for the Swallows Partnership between the Swallows Foundation UK and Issaseko Senkonjani, and performed at Port Elizabeth Opera House; thanks to Peter Stark, Peggy Calata, Michael Barry, Zamuxolo Mgoduka, OyamoVanto and Gcobani Poltini, and the other riders of the bus. 'At the top of the tree, keep climbing' was written as part of a project for Cleveland Community Forest.

'Home as a cornucopia' was originally part of 21 Ways of Looking at the Sponsors Club, commissioned by The Sponsors Club; thanks to Adam Lopardo. 'On making' was originally written for rednile projects' 'Factory Nights'; thanks to them for commissioning the essay which sparked its argument with Albert Goldbarth's 'Beauty'.

Some of the Dunno Elegies were written with specific people in mind, or as dedicatees. I is for Mick Henry, II for Joe Doherty, III for Alan Davey who gave me the first line by mistyping a text, VI for Canon Bill Hall.

The poems in the section from *Half A Mind* are all from a long sequence called 'Bringing Down The Government'. A small number of other poems originally published in *Half A Mind* found new homes in the sequences 'How I Learned To Sing' and 'Esperanto Anonyme'.